Looking Back at Bristol Channel Shipping

by

Andrew Wiltshire

The **Hazelmoor** was a splendid looking general cargo vessel built in 1954 by Hawthorn Leslie at Hebburn, the year after her sister-ship **Glenmoor**. She had a gross tonnage of 5572 and was delivered to Moor Line Ltd of Newcastle-upon-Tyne, a long established company managed and owned by Walter Runciman and Co Ltd. The **Hazelmoor** is constructed to a fairly common layout, often referred to as being split-superstructure, whereby her No. 3 hold aft of her bridge and forward of her funnel was flanked by accommodation. She is powered by a 4-cylinder Hawthorn Leslie built Doxford engine developing 3300bhp. Her masts are of the telescopic type to allow her to transit the Manchester Ship Canal. This series of vessels continued with the **Innesmoor** in 1954

followed by the **Jedmoor** and **Linkmoor** in 1958 and 1961 respectively. In 1968 Moor Line ceased and Walter Runciman transferred ownership of the fleet to a newly-created Anchor Line Ship Management Ltd. The **Glenmoor**, **Hazelmoor** and **Linkmoor** gained Anchor Line's colours of a grey hull and black funnel. The **Hazelmoor** is seen arriving at Cardiff on 31 May 1975 with a cargo of bone chippings from India. These would be used to make gelatine at the P J Leiner factory in Treforest. The **Hazelmoor** was sold in 1978 to Hesperus Navigation Corp, of Panama, and became **Freddie I** and was sold for breaking up at Gadani Beach, Pakistan, later the same year.

(John Wiltshire)

Introduction

My first book, *Bristol Channel Shipping Memories*, was well received by many and subsequently I have been encouraged to think about putting together a sequel. This book, therefore, takes a further look at shipping in the Bristol Channel in the years when vessels were still plentiful and variety abounded. This time our journey will begin in North Devon and head along the coast to the River Avon and its adjacent ports, before moving on to Sharpness and a trip along the canal to Gloucester. Heading down the Severn and into South Wales, we eventually reach Swansea.

New locations featured include Watchet, Gloucester and Sharpness as well as the then newly-opened tidal harbour at Port Talbot. Along the way we will see a tremendous cross section of ship types including coasters discharging at riverside wharves, passenger excursion vessels, a dredger at work and even a warship. As is usual practice, and throughout this book, the gross registered tonnage of most of the vessels is given, eg 3456grt, and deadweight as dwt. Horsepower is shown as bhp (brake horsepower), ihp (indicated horsepower) and shp (shaft horsepower).

Andrew Wiltshire   Cardiff   February 2010

Acknowledgements

Having been given the go-ahead to produce *Looking Back at Bristol Chann Shipping*, I have had the pleasure over the winter of 2008/9 of gathering togeth a further selection of slides from my regular sources. I would like to thank r father John Wiltshire for allowing me to delve into his vast collection of slides on again. A big thank you must also go to Bob Allen and Nigel Jones for taking tin to put together some superb shots for me to consider for inclusion in the boc Derek Chaplin very kindly lent me his collection of shipping slides so that I cou select any subjects for use in future titles, and this source has proved to be ve valuable. Danny Lynch and John Woodward have also very kindly let me u some of their work, whilst my good friend Kevin Blair with assistance from Pa Hood, has tirelessly slaved away checking details of ships large and small that a featured in the book. Thanks also to Chris Jones for the extra details on t *Robert A*. As always, Bernard McCall has kept the book on a steady cour throughout its preparation and Gil Mayes has again checked several drafts of t book. Written sources used throughout include *Lloyd's Register of Shipping*, *Co Towage* (by W J Harvey), various editions of *Ocean Ships* and *Ships Montl* magazine and various editions of *Merchant Ships World* (by Adlard Coles Ltc Once again I must thank Amadeus Press for their consistently high standard reproduction.

Published by: Bernard McCall, 400 Nore Road, Portishead, Bristol, BS20 8EZ, England. Website: www.coastalshipping.co.uk
Telephone/fax: 01275 846178; e-mail: bernard@coastalshipping.co.uk. All distribution enquiries should be addressed to the publisher.

Printed by Amadeus Press, Ezra House, West 26 Business Park, Cleckheaton, West Yorkshire, BD19 4TQ.
Telephone: 01274 863210; fax: 01274 863211; e-mail: info@amadeuspress.co.uk; website: www.amadeuspress.co.uk   ISBN: 978-1-902953-46-5

Front cover: The River Avon in the Avon Gorge was for over a century a classic setting for ship photography with many hundreds of vessels being recorded passing this location. The cargo ship *Gertrud Bratt* is nearing the end of her journey up to the City Docks at Bristol in April 1967. To ensure a safe passage, the local King tug *John King* is secured to her bow. At this point the ensemble is about to pass under the Clifton Suspension Bridge, with the Portway in the background, to reach the lock at the Cumberland Basin and enter the dock system itself. It is highly likely that the *Gertrud Bratt* has arrived from the Baltic with timber and paper products. She is 1530grt, and was built in 1957 in Belgium by Brugeoise S.A. for Angfartygs ab Adolf of Gothenburg, though by the time this view was taken she was operating for Salen Lines Ltd also of Gothenburg. Later in 1967, the *Gertrud Bratt* became *Carmen* for Martinez Pereira y Cia, of Valparaiso, under the Chilean flag. On 12 October 1977, whilst sailing between Mazatlan and Guaymas, she was beached at Punta San Ignacia, Mexico, and became a wreck. The motor tug *John King* dated from 1936 and was built locally by Charles Hill at Bristol. She left King ownership in 1970, and after several local owners, is now preserved as a working exhibit at the Bristol Industrial Museum.

(Derek Chaplin)

Back cover: A distinctive class of four refrigerated cargo ships was delivered 1966 to Federal Lines and New Zealand Shipping. The first completed was th *Westmorland* for Federal Lines Ltd, followed by the *Taupo*, *Tekoa* an *Tongariro* for the New Zealand Shipping Company Ltd. They introduced a ne hull colour officially described as "eau-de-nil" and Hallen derricks were deploye throughout for the first time. The latter were controlled by a joystick and include four 10-ton, three 15-ton booms and a single 30-ton boom. Cargo spac comprised five holds mostly insulated, with upper and lower tween deck 475,000 cubic feet of which was suitable for refrigerated cargo, and in additic there were four cargo tanks. The *Westmorland* was built on the Clyde, but th three Ts were completed by Bartram and Sons Ltd at Sunderland. The *Tongarir* is seen arriving at Swansea on 13 June 1968, possibly for a visit to the dry-doc She was 8233grt, 528 feet in length and had a service speed in excess of 1 knots. Crew was normally forty-seven, but a further ten could be catered for, all air-conditioned quarters. Federal became her official owners in 1969 and she wa later merged into the P&O fleet along with her sisters. She was sold in 1979 an became the *Reefer Princess* under the Greek flag. At less than twenty years age, she was broken up in 1985 at Gadani Beach.

(John Wiltshir

We begin our journey at the North Devon resort of Ilfracombe. Building on the success of the paddle steamer *Waverley*, the Firth of Clyde Steam Packet Co Ltd, a group associated with the Paddle Steamer Preservation Society, purchased the fine looking motor vessel *Shanklin* from Sealink in 1980, and renamed her *Prince Ivanhoe*. She arrived on the Clyde in November the same year for renovation. As *Shanklin* she was the final member of a class of three similar passenger vessels built for British Railways (Southern Region) Portsmouth to Ryde service. The two earlier vessels were the well-known *Southsea* and *Brading*, both of 1948. Built by William Denny & Bros, of Dumbarton, the *Shanklin* was delivered in 1951 and was 833grt. She was a twin-screw ship powered by a pair of Sulzer diesels, and despite being the newest she was the first of the trio to be withdrawn with engine trouble and put up for sale. As the *Prince Ivanhoe* she was to prove very popular in the Bristol Channel, and we see her just off Ilfracombe on 1 August 1981. Tragically, two days later she struck a submerged object off Port Eynon on the Gower peninsular. Taking on water, she was quickly run up onto the nearby beach to prevent her sinking in deep water, and thus averting a catastrophe. All 450 passengers on board were saved, and on 5 August she was declared a constructive total loss, the wreck later being broken up where it lay.

(Nigel Jones)

The Isles of Scilly Steamship Co Ltd replaced its 1925-built steam passenger ship **Scillonian** with a smart new motor vessel in 1956. She too was named **Scillonian** and the steam vessel was subsequently broken up. The new ship was completed by the Southampton shipyard of John I Thornycroft & Co Ltd and could accommodate 500 passengers. She had a gross tonnage of 921 and was a twin-screw vessel powered by a pair of 6-cylinder Ruston & Hornsby diesels and capable of 15 knots. After 21 years service plying between Penzance and the Isles of Scilly, she was replaced by a larger ship in 1977. The **Scillonian** was purchased by P & A Campbell in 1977 for £150,000 and renamed **Devonia**. It was the intention to use her on the Thames and the Bristol Channel, with a view to utilising her freight capability on a service to Lundy Island, and here she is seen off Ilfracombe on 2 July 1977. She saw little use between 1978 and 1980 and when P & A Campbell ceased trading, the vessel remained laid up until 1982, when she passed to Torbay Seaways as the **Devoniun**. Two years later she became **Syllingar** of Norse Atlantic Ferries for about a year, and after several changes of name, she worked in the Mediterranean and off West Africa. As the **Olga J.** and under the Belize flag, she was arrested at Haifa, Israel, in 1998 for being in an unseaworthy state. In what can only be described as an act of defiance, she broke out of the port under the cover of darkness and ended up at at Bourgos in Bulgaria, where she was abandoned by her crew and later sank.

(Nigel Jones)

We now move up channel into Somerset to call at the small port of Watchet. Having just arrived at the East Quay in the harbour with a deck cargo of timber, the Dutch flag **Breezand** is being made secure alongside in July 1969. Watchet is an ancient town with its roots going back over one thousand years. Over the years the harbour has seen the export of iron ore from the nearby Brendon Hills as well as more recently the import of wood products for Watchet paper mill. It closed as a commercial port in 1993, but remains active as a marina. Steeped in history, Watchet remains a popular spot for tourists and the town boasts other attractions such as the West Somerset Railway passing through on its way to Minehead. The coaster **Breezand** was launched by Kerstholt Scheeps NV of Groningen in October 1961 and delivered in 1962 to P A van Es & Co. N.V. The **Breezand** was 499grt and became the **Aat V** in 1973, still under the Dutch flag and by 1984 was operating for Ikaros Shipping of Greece as the **Dedalos**. It was in this guise that she collided with a pier at Aliveri on 1 April 1987 and sank. She was later raised and broken up at Perama near Piraeus.

(Derek Chaplin)

Dunball Wharf is located on the River Parrett in Somerset and close to the small port of Bridgwater. The wharf was built by local coal merchants in 1844 and was adjacent to the village of Dunball. Until 1962 it was served by rail traffic and evidence of this is still visible in this view of the coasters *Pavonis* and *Rose* taken in June 1966. After the Second World War the wharf was used to import fertiliser for use locally, and also Welsh coal for the Royal Ordnance Factory at Puriton. In more recent times it has been used to land sand and gravel mainly for use in the building industry. The *Pavonis* was a Dutch coaster of 384grt and built in 1960 by Fikkers of Foxhol, and was working for Rederij Salomons & Wildeman, of Groningen, at the time of this photograph. The further vessel is the *Rose* of 1956 owned by N.V. Scheepvaart-Onderneming Kustverkeer and registered in Rotterdam. She was larger than the *Pavonis* at 497grt and after her sale in 1970 became a wine tanker named *Gleucosin* for Italian owners at Genoa. By 1983 she had become a water tanker for the same owner, Armammento M/c "Gleucos", and is still active in 2009 under the same name but with Zole CE of Marsala, Sicily.

(Derek Chaplin)

Battery Point at Portishead was and indeed still is a good vantage point to watch shipping sailing to and from the Bristol area ports. Outbound from Avonmouth in June 1971 is T & J Harrison's **Adventurer** of 1960. She was the first British ship to be fitted with a Stülcken heavy lift derrick and with a capacity of 180 tons was the heaviest of its kind in the world at this time. The derrick dominates this view of her and we can study her unusual layout with bridge accommodation amidships and her machinery situated ahead of her No.5 cargo hold. The **Adventurer** was followed in 1961 by the similar **Custodian** and **Tactician**. She was 8971grt and built by Doxford at the Pallion Yard in Sunderland, being launched on 21 May 1959. She had a 6-cylinder Doxford diesel of 6800bhp and a service speed of around 15 knots, and when delivered her actual owner was listed as Charente S. S. Co, of Liverpool. The **Adventurer** became the **Eleftheria** for Prospel Maritime Ltd of Greece in 1980 and was broken up at Gadani Beach in 1985. Liverpool-based T & J Harrison's interests in shipping dated back to 1853 and in 1970 they were still operating services from the UK to South America, the West Indies and South Africa/Mozambique. By 1988 the company owned just three vessels due to the general decline in British shipping, and has now withdrawn from the industry altogether.

(Derek Chaplin)

The **Bristol Queen** was the first of two modern and stylish post war paddlesteamers built for service with P & A Campbell Ltd. She was launched on 4 April 1946 by Charles Hill and Sons, of Bristol, and delivered in the following September. The **Bristol Queen** was 961grt and had a triple expansion, 3-crank diagonal engine of 2700ihp built by Rankin and Blackmore. Like her near sistership **Cardiff Queen** she was built with oil-fired boilers. We see her passing Portishead and heading down channel in July 1967, at the end of her career. After a poor season the **Bristol Queen** was taken out of service on 26 August 1967, following damage to a paddle wheel, and was laid up at Cardiff. While moored in the Queen Alexandra Dock on 14 January 1968, and in high winds, she was struck by the tanker **Geodor** and damaged. Shortly after this she was sold to a Belgian breaker and towed away on 21 March by the German tug **Fairplay XII** for scrapping at Willebroek in Belgium.

(Derek Chaplin)

The **Harry Brown** was a sand dredger and a familiar sight in the Bristol Channel for many years. She was delivered to Holms Sand and Gravel Co, a subsidiary of T R Brown & Sons of Bristol, in 1962 by Charles Hill's shipyard and was 634grt. She was a suction dredger and her main cargo pumps were electrically driven. She replaced the old dredger **Sandholm** of 1920, and was put to work alongside the steam powered dredger **Steep Holm**. The **Harry Brown** is seen passing Portishead in March 1972 most probably bound for the City Docks with a cargo of sand. In 1978 Holms Sand and Gravel became part of the Bristol Sand and Gravel Co, a joint venture with British Dredging. This business along with the **Harry Brown** passed to ARC Marine Ltd UK in 1986, and she continued to bring sand into Bristol until 1990. After 28 years in the Channel, the **Harry Brown** passed to Hellebore Ltd, of Waterford, and in January 1991 she was sold to buyers in the Middle East. Renamed **Alwardi 4** she departed for Bahrain the following month. In 1992 she became **Sabah** and then **Salaiti 17** for Salaiti Marine Services of Bahrain in 1995. She is thought to be still in service as such in 2010.

(Derek Chaplin)

Our next port of call is the dock at Portishead. The **Corstream** was a fine looking steam collier belonging to Wm. Cory and Son Ltd whose funnel markings were a very familiar sight on the River Thames, the area which it regularly visited with coal from the north-east coast of England. She was built in 1955 by the Burntisland Shipbuilding Co Ltd, of Burntisland, on the east coast of Scotland, and was 3375grt. She had a pair of 220psi three-furnace, oil-fired boilers and was driven by a North Eastern "reheat" triple expansion engine of 1100ihp. The **Corstream** had five hopper-sided holds designed for chute loading and grab discharge.. She is seen here at Portishead laid up in the autumn sunshine in November 1971. In 1972 her registered owner was Liquid Gas Tankers Ltd, but that year she was sold to Kieland Shipping Co Ltd of Cyprus and became the **Kyramaruko**. This new guise was to be short-lived as she went aground on the Horns Reef while sailing from Gdansk to Esbjerg and received serious hull damage. She arrived at Hamburg under tow in January 1973 to be scrapped.

(Derek Chaplin)

Portishead dock dates from the 1860s, and in 1880 it was acquired by Bristol Corporation. Albright & Wilson Ltd built a chemical plant at Portishead in 1951 to produce white phosphorus from imported phosphate rock, with power for the furnaces coming from the power station on the opposite side of the dock. Most of the coal for the power station was brought from South Wales by local ships, while the rock arrived by ship in liquid form from Long Harbour in Newfoundland. Out of interest, the only other discharge point in the world for this type of cargo was Kinura Ko in Japan. The **Albright Pioneer** was one of a pair of chemical carriers built in 1968 for Albright and Wilson Manufacturing Ltd, the second ship being the **Albright Explorer**. The **Albright Pioneer** was completed by Vickers at High Walker on the River Tyne and together with her sistership was to be managed by James Fisher & Sons Ltd, of Barrow-in-Furness, and registered in Newcastle. The **Albright Pioneer** had a pair of Deutz diesels that were geared to a single controllable-pitch propeller and gave a speed of 14 knots. Her dimensions were 414 feet overall and 57 feet beam, her gross tonnage being 6789. In 1990 she was converted to a cargo ship by removing her cargo tanks, and renamed **Bright Pioneer**. She became **Brigitte** in 1991 and **Searaider** in 1994. She was broken up at Aliaga in February 2001 as the **Raider**. On a sunny 13 July 1969 we see the **Albright Pioneer** moored at the Albright & Wilson wharf.

(John Wiltshire)

Besides coal and phosphate other cargoes to arrive in Portishead by sea included refined oils, timber and wood pulp. The small German flag cargo ship **Sabine Howaldt** is seen entering Portishead dock under the guidance of the Cardiff based tug **Danegarth** in June 1968. This was unusual, and there must have been a lot of shipping movements at Avonmouth that tide, thus requiring a tug to be sent across from the South Wales port to help out at Portishead. The **Danegarth** was transferred to Newport in 1979 and sold to Greek owners in 1992. The **Sabine Howaldt** was built in 1958 by Nobiskrug at Rendsburg where she was launched on 11 March 1958 for Howaldt & Co. She was 2288grt, powered by a Deutz engine and had a service speed of 12 knots. Her cargo facilities consisted of two large holds serviced by ten derricks. In 1971 she became the Greek-owned **Eusthatia** and in 1985 became the **Pal** for Loup Maritime Corp under the Honduran flag. She was broken up after arriving at Gadani Beach in September 1985. The dock at Portishead finally closed to commercial traffic in 1992, the power station being demolished in 1997, and the Albright & Wilson works followed in 2000.

(Derek Chaplin)

The port at Avonmouth was built on the north-eastern bank of the River Avon at its mouth. On her final approaches to Avonmouth, the Royal Mail Lines cargo liner *Darro* will continue to reduce speed before turning to port and through 270 degrees whilst picking up her tugs in the process. This is an early morning shot on 28 December 1976 and the *Darro* has arrived from Australia with a cargo of dairy produce. By this date Royal Mail Lines had virtually disappeared as a separate entity, having been taken over by Furness Withy and Company in 1965. The *Darro* had been transferred within this group, and was originally with Shaw Savill where she had carried the name *Carnatic*. As such she was launched on 11 July 1956 by Cammell Laird at Birkenhead and had a gross tonnage of 11144. She was a twin-screw fast refrigerated cargo ship with a pair of 6-cylinder built B&W diesels built by Harland & Wolff; these were capable of producing 14300bhp and gave a speed of 18 knots. In 1969 she transferred to Crusader Shipping retaining her name *Carnatic*, before becoming the *Darro* in 1973. Her sisterships *Cretic* and *Cymric* also passed to Royal Mail Lines at around this time. The *Darro* passed to Greek owners in 1977 as *Litsa K.* and to Taiwanese breakers in June 1979 as *Dimitra* also under the Greek flag.

(John Wiltshire)

Palm Line had its origins with detergent and soap manufacturer William Lever who sourced palm oil from West Africa. The United Africa Company was formed in 1929 and went on to become Palm Line in 1949. Ships of Palm Line sailed from the UK to West African ports and were regularly seen in the Bristol Channel. They acquired their first new vessels in 1952. The **Ibadan Palm** was built at the Swan Hunter shipyard on the Tyne and completed in September 1959, followed three months later by her sistership **Ilorin Palm**. She had 5 holds as well as deep tanks suitable for carrying vegetable oils and her air-conditioned accommodation provided facilities for two passengers. Bipod masts were to feature for the first time on the **Ibadan Palm**. She was 5799grt and had a 4-cylinder

Doxford engine which gave her a service speed of 14 knots. She is seen in the oil dock at Avonmouth on 1 September 1972 waiting for a berth, and with large hardwood logs visible on deck. In 1978 Palm Line sold the **Ibadan Palm** to Kuwait interests who named her **Hind** and the following year she passed to Hind Shipping Co Ltd, of Hong Kong, as **Arunkamal**. She was broken up at Gadani Beach, where she arrived in January 1983. Her sistership **Ilorin Palm** was sold for scrapping in Bangladesh a month earlier. At its peak in 1962 Palm Line had 23 vessels including a trio of vegetable oil tankers, but in 1985 the business was sold to Ocean Transport and on to French owners in 1989.

(John Wiltshire)

The **Benya River** was a fine looking general cargo ship belonging to the Ghanaian flag Black Star Line Ltd of Takoradi, and named after a river in the south of that country. She was one of a series of fourteen similar motor ships and was delivered in 1965, the last of four built by Swan Hunter and Wigham Richardson at Wallsend on the Tyne. The lead vessel was the **Sakumo Lagoon**, ordered in 1963, and like the following two ships had accommodation for 12 passengers. The **Benya River**, however, was to be the Black Star Line flagship and featured a special and very elaborate suite for Dr Kwame Nkrumah, the President of Ghana. Her cargo facilities included special provision for carrying large logs

and her derricks included one each of 25 ton and 60 ton capacity. These ships had an overall length of 454 feet and a beam of 62 feet and the main engine was a 6-cylinder Sulzer of 7200bhp built by the Wallsend shipyard which gave a service speed of 17 knots. The **Benya River** is seen arriving at Avonmouth on a fine morning on 20 April 1976. She became **Water Wealth** in 1985 and **Jah** later that year. In 1987 she regained the name **Water Wealth** and sailed to Indian breakers as such in November 1988.

(John Wiltshire)

Departing the lock at Avonmouth in May 1975 is the coastal tanker **Esso Hythe**. She was built in 1959 by Henry Scarr at Hessle for the Esso Petroleum Co Ltd, and was very similar to the **Esso Lyndhurst** of 1958. She had eight cargo tanks that were heated by steam coils and a deadweight tonnage of 1285. The **Esso Hythe** as the name might suggest was built primarily for the Southampton Water bunkering fleet. She was 208 feet in length and her accommodation was for up to eighteen officers and crew. She was powered by an 8-cylinder English Electric diesel with an output of 750bhp at 675rpm.

Away from the Solent, she would regularly turn up in the Bristol Channel visiting, besides Avonmouth, the Esso terminal on the Ely River at Cardiff as well providing fuel oil bunkers to ships at the South Wales ports. She became **Rim** in 1981 for Tristar Shipping, of Tripoli, under the Lebanese flag and later **Rima I** in 1998 for Ali Kara Hassan under the Belize flag. Remarkably she is still believed to be trading in 2010 but *Lloyd's Register* gives no details of owner or even flag.

(Derek Chaplin)

The tramp ship **Egton** was one of only two post war motor vessels delivered to Whitby based Headlam and Son, and was completed in 1962 with a grt of 7175. Her builder was Bartram of South Dock, Sunderland, and she had a 4-cylinder Doxford oil engine which gave her a speed of 14 knots. The **Egton** was named after a peaceful village on the North Yorkshire Moors and was a ship that seemed to spend a large part of her 24 years existence laid up rather than earning her keep. Initially she was laid up at Sunderland for fourteen months after completion by her builder and also spent further periods of lay-up at Leith and again at Sunderland. To make matters worse, on 24 January 1967, after leaving dry-dock on the Tees, she ran aground off Whitby. She ended up in dry-dock at Wallsend to be checked over and whilst her tanks were being drained of oil, a fire started causing more damage to her hull. She eventually sailed for China in July of 1967 and continued to trade once more. Her final spell in lay-up was to commence on 24 April 1977 when she arrived at Hartlepool Here the **Egton** was to become a local landmark, as she remained at her berth for nearly nine years because her owner refused to sell her. The story goes that apparently Bill Headlam announced that "as long as he was alive he'd be a shipowner". Eventually she was sold for scrapping in Finland and was towed away by the tug **Formidable**, arriving at Naantali on 18 January 1986. She visited Avonmouth in 1969 where she is seen at one of the grain berths on 14 July.

(John Wiltshire)

The cargo ship **Chrysovalandou Dyo** was completed as **Eastern Trader** in February 1959 for Indo-China Steam Navigation Co Ltd (Jardine Matheson & Co Ltd) with whom she had been employed on the Hong Kong to Australia run. She was constructed by Swan Hunter at their Low Walker yard and was 6914grt. She had an overall length of 481 feet and 62 feet beam; her 5-cylinder Doxford engine gave a speed of 14 knots. She was renamed **Chrysovalandou Dyo** in 1972 when she was purchased by Santiren Shipping Co Ltd under the Cypriot flag and nine years later in April 1981 arrived at Gadani Beach to be dismantled by Pakistani shipbreakers. It was quite common to see nearly all the berths at Avonmouth fully occupied, but to find ships berthed two abreast was very unusual indeed. Also in this view dated 14 January 1973 we can see Harrison Lines' **Historian** of 1968 moored on the inside, whilst astern of the **Chrysovalandou Dyo** is a cargo vessel belonging to the Pakistan National Shipping Corporation and an East German flag freighter.

(John Wiltshire)

Ships of the Blue Star Line were frequent callers at Avonmouth in the 1960s. Blue Star Line was formed by the Liverpool-based Vestey Brothers in 1909 and registered in 1911. The intention was to import meat produce and other perishables to the UK, and its first refrigerated ships had appeared by 1913. Trade grew and services to Australia, New Zealand, South Africa and South America soon materialised. One of the older members of the fleet in 1970 was the 11085grt **Empire Star** of 1946. She is seen moored in the passage area of King Edward dock on 28 August 1970. She was launched on 4 March 1946 as **Empire Mercia** by Harland and Wolff at Belfast for the Ministry of Transport.

However, she was completed in December 1946 as the **Empire Star** for Frederick Leyland & Co with Blue Star Line as managers. She was a twin-screw refrigerated cargo ship, 521 feet in length and 70 feet in the beam, and her main engines were a pair of complex 8-cylinder Burmeister and Wain oil engines assembled by Harland & Wolff. These engines were of the double-acting opposed-piston type and were very unpopular with the engineering staff, especially in later years when reliability became more of an issue. In October 1971 she arrived at Kaohsiung to be broken up having been purchased by Long Jong Industrial Co Ltd.

(John Wiltshire)

In 1972 Bristol tug operator C J King and Sons still operated two steam powered vessels in their Avonmouth-based fleet, and both were Empire type tugs dating from the Second World War. To replace the coal-burning **Sea Alarm** of 1941, the King company bought the motor tug **Foreman** from United Towing, of Hull, in 1973. Despite being built in 1959, she had an outdated appearance with the lines of a steam tug complete with a tall funnel. She was taken to Charles Hill's yard in Bristol and modernised with a new wheelhouse and funnel. She emerged as the **Sea Bristolian** and was put to work at Avonmouth, but was also used for coastal towing from time to time. Built at the Beverley yard of Cook, Welton and Gemmell, she had an 8-cylinder Ruston & Hornsby engine of 1200ihp. In this view on 10 February 1973, she is in charge of the **Troyberg**, a German owned cargo ship sailing under the Liberian flag. Having been replaced at Avonmouth by the new tug the **Sea Endeavour**, the **Sea Bristolian** was sold in 1981 to Dubai owners and renamed **Mansco Tug 4**. Whilst on her delivery voyage on 2 October 1981 she ran aground in Pontevedra Bay, near Vigo whilst bound for Piraeus; both tug and tow were lost in this incident.

(John Wiltshire)

The **Robert A.** worked for the local lighterage operator Ashmead & Son Ltd based in Bristol, and would normally be found at Avonmouth or the City Docks moored among the barges. On 28 March 1969 she is seen leaving the lock at Avonmouth with an unladen barge in tow. The **Robert A.** may be small but she is quite a special tug. She was delivered to C J King & Sons in 1934 as the **Volunteer**, the first motor tug to appear in the Bristol Channel. Built locally by Charles Hill & Sons at Bristol, she started life with a 4-cylinder Petter diesel of 203bhp, which was later replaced with a British Polar diesel of 350bhp. She passed to Ashmead in 1959 as **Robert A.** The King company took delivery of a second motor tug in 1936, the slightly larger **John King** (see cover), which incidentally passed to Ashmead in 1970 as the **Peter Leigh**. Ashmead sold the **Robert A.** in 1983 to Drake Towage, of Wisbech, who named her **Sea Fitter**. Wisbech-based Mr Akroyd then took her on and renamed her **Robert A.** once again. In 2002 she made the long trip to Whitehaven in Cumbria where Patterson Boatworks intended to convert her into a yacht named **Volunteer**. This did not happen and she was later sold on to another private buyer, who plans to return the vessel to Bristol for restoration.

(John Wiltshire)

The **Nyanza** was built for the British India Steam Navigation Co in 1956 by Scotts of Greenock. She was a steam turbine powered cargo ship of 8513grt and her Parsons turbines which developed 11275shp were assembled by Scotts, which in turn gave her a speed of 17 knots. Her main role was to trade between the UK and Australia with general cargo. In 1964 she was transferred to P&O and renamed **Balranald** until 1968 when she reverted to **Nyanza** once more for British India. She is seen having just arrived in the lock at Avonmouth on 3 February 1974, and by this time she had gained the corporate P&O funnel colours which did little to enhance her appearance. The P&O houseflag is clearly seen flying on her jackstay. She was sold in 1974 to Arya National Shipping Line, of Iran, and renamed **Arya Gol**. Being steam-powered she would have been an expensive vessel to operate, and it came as no surprise to see her sold for scrap to Pakistani breakers in 1976.

(John Wiltshire)

The British India Steam Navigation Co Ltd. took delivery of 5 similar refrigerated motor cargo ships between 1959 and 1961. They were intended for the Australia to India and Persian Gulf trade and included the **Bulimba** of 1959 and **Bombala** of 1961. Their design was a departure from tradition, and all five ships had four cargo holds served by a mixture of derricks and electrically driven cranes. All accommodation was air conditioned and included an owner's cabin which could be used for two passengers. The **Bulimba** is seen at Avonmouth on 17 October 1970, her name coming from a town on the Brisbane River in Queensland, Australia. She was built by Harland and Wolff at Govan on the Clyde, who also assembled her 6-cylinder opposed-piston Burmeister & Wain 6700bhp main engine. She was 6791grt and all five vessels in the class used alternating current for all electrical installations on board, the first example of this in a British-built ship. After only twelve years service the **Bulimba** was sold in 1971 to the Malaysian International Shipping Corporation and renamed **Bunga Kenanga**. In 1977 she became **Seasprite**, initially under the Liberian flag and then the Greek flag. Two years later on 30 June 1979 the vessel became a total loss after running aground in Kori Creek in the Gulf of Kutch in India. She was subsequently abandoned.

(John Wiltshire)

At nineteen years of age, the impressive looking *Centaur* was something of a stranger to UK waters. She was launched on 20 June 1963 by John Brown and Co (Clydebank) Ltd of Glasgow for Blue Funnel's Port Swettenham-Singapore-Fremantle service, and was 8262grt with an overall length of 481 feet. With a service speed of 20 knots, she was Blue Funnel's first post-war motor vessel with twin-screw propulsion. As a passenger vessel with accommodation for 190, the *Centaur* featured such luxuries as stabilisers and a swimming pool but could also cater for 4500 sheep or 700 cattle. In addition to general cargo she could carry refrigerated produce as well as palm oil and latex in special tanks. In 1975 she was transferred to Eastern Fleets Ltd of Singapore and then three years later to Blue Funnel (S.E. Asia) Private Ltd. The *Centaur* was withdrawn from service in 1981 and in 1982 chartered by the St. Helena Shipping Co Ltd. to cover for their own vessel *St. Helena* which had been requisitioned for service in the Falklands war. The *Centaur* was sold to Chinese owner The Shanghai Haixing Shipping Co in 1985 and renamed *Hai Long*. In 1986 this was changed to *Hai Da* and nine years later she arrived at the Xinhui scrapyard in China for breaking up. We see her sailing from Avonmouth on 20 May 1983.

(Nigel Jones)

Here we have another fine looking ship, for which sadly, time was running out. In May 1968, the Cardiff-registered *Newglade* of 1944 is arriving at Avonmouth on an afternoon tide. Despite her attractive and traditional lines, the condition of the *Newglade* can only be described as a sorry state. She was completed nearly twenty-four years earlier in November 1944 as the *Brockleymoor* for Moor Line Ltd, of Newcastle, which was a subsidiary of ship owner Walter Runciman. The location Brockleymoor is a small hamlet near Plumpton in Cumbria. As *Brockleymoor* she was built at the Pallion yard of Doxford in Sunderland with a 3-cylinder Doxford oil engine and a gross tonnage of 7368. In 1960 she passed to John Cory and Sons Ltd and was renamed *Restormel* and registered in Cardiff. Four years later she was sold to the Waterloo Shipping Co Ltd and kept her Cardiff port of registry and took the name *Newglade*, and the funnel markings of Tsavliris Shipping. On 7 November, a few months after this photograph was taken, she caught fire at Kynosoura on the Greek island of Salamis and was eventually sold for scrap in 1969.

(Bob Allen)

Bristol Corporation took delivery of an effluents tanker from the Ailsa shipyard at Troon in 1969. She was launched on 12 June 1968 and delivered as the **Glen Avon** in September 1969. She was 859grt and was a twin-screw vessel propelled by a pair of 6-cylinder Ruston and Hornsby diesels of 1510bhp. Her main duty was to transport sewerage from a loading point on the north bank of the River Avon for discharge at sea in the deeper waters of the Bristol Channel. She has just entered the River Avon in this view taken on 26 March 1973 with Portishead power station in the distance, and will make her way slowly up towards Bristol. This ship was a part of the local scene for about 25 years, but because of her somewhat less than glamorous role was often overlooked. Ownership passed to the Wessex Water Authority in about 1975, when they took over the role performed by Bristol Corporation's water works department. The **Glen Avon** was made redundant in 1993 following changes in legislation, which saw the dumping of effluent at sea regarded as environmentally undesirable. She was subsequently sold and became the **Olokun 2** in 1994 for Marine and Oil International Ltd under the Nigerian flag who, it is believed, used her as a conventional tanker. She was converted at Sharpness.

(John Wiltshire)

The city docks at Bristol are located alongside the River Avon about three miles upstream from Avonmouth. The elderly Scandinavian steamship **Vard** was built in 1930 as **Lido** for Norwegian owner D/S A/S Laly (Gogstad), of Oslo. She was constructed as a 1918grt cargo ship with a length of 283 feet and a breadth of 42 feet, by the Nylands Verksted shipyard in Oslo. From new she was fitted with one of this yard's own compound steam engines of 800ihp. Twenty-four years later in 1954 she passed to Egil Naesheims Rederi A/S, another Norwegian ship-owner who named her **Vard**. Her lines were very traditional and this view taken late one afternoon in September 1970 shows she is still in very good condition externally. She is moored alongside Wapping Wharf and is in Bristol with a cargo of Scandinavian timber. Despite her remarkable condition, she was to end her days just four months later at a breaker's yard in Flushing in January 1971.

(Derek Chaplin)

The **Ionion Pelagos** was a Greek-owned steamship dating from 1949 and built in the United Kingdom. Her builders, Smiths Dock Co Ltd of South Bank, Middlesbrough, completed her in March 1949 as the 2047grt **Mafalda** for A/S Norsk Transatlantic, of Oslo. She was 326 feet long with four cargo holds, and had a 4-cylinder compound steam engine assembled by Smith's Dock and a speed of 11 knots. In 1962 she was sold to Finnish owners Rederi A/B Yrsa and renamed **Yrsa**. After just four years in that role she became the **Ionion Pelagos**, as we see her here at Canons Marsh, Bristol, in June 1968, waiting to discharge. The paintwork on her hull appears to be receiving some attention while in port. Her new owners were Viagrande Cia. Nav. S.A. and they had registered her in Piraeus. Sadly this fine looking ship was wrecked at Ormos Agios Annas, Mykonos, on 28 March 1971. The quayside behind the ship had changed beyond all recognition by 2010, and now features apartment blocks and modern offices.

(Derek Chaplin)

The General Steam Navigation Co Ltd was originally founded in 1824 and by the 1960s operated a fleet of about forty ships, including a number of small passenger vessels. Most of the ships were to be found trading mainly between London and the near Continent and the Mediterranean. The majority of the fleet were named after birds and the *Grebe* is a fine example of a small coastal cargo ship built in 1948. She was 933grt and completed in June of that year by Henry Robb Ltd, of Leith. The *Grebe* was a motor ship fitted with a 1200bhp British Polar diesel and her principal dimensions were 235 feet overall length, 37 feet 4 inch beam with a draught of 13 feet 10 inches when laden. She is seen discharging at St Augustines Reach, Bristol, in September 1966, and her condition gives the impression she is a little uncared for. Her days would be brought to an end in the Bristol Channel as she was delivered to John Cashmore at Newport on 18 October 1967 for breaking up. In 1920 a controlling stake was obtained in General Steam Navigation by P&O, and by 1972 competition had forced them out of business.

(Derek Chaplin)

William Sloan and Co Ltd, of Glasgow, operated a coastal liner service from that city to ports such as Belfast, Bristol, Cardiff and Swansea. Cargoes carried included tobacco and often a call was made at Dublin. Bristol was an important centre for the tobacco industry with names like Wills and Imperial Tobacco having a large presence in the city. William Sloan was taken over by Coast Lines in the late 1950s and at this point the steam vessels left the fleet. Motor ships at this time had a black hull with white superstructure and by the mid-1960s included the **Tay**, **Kelvin** and **Talisker**. The latter was acquired in 1963 and is seen here at Cripps Corner, Bristol, in February 1967 having some of her paintwork touched up. A number of containers can be seen as deck cargo. The **Talisker** was built in 1955 by George Brown, of Greenock, as **Ulster Pioneer** for the Belfast Steamship Company. She was 1016grt and her Sulzer main engine was built by G Clark. The business was later merged with Burns and Laird and the **Talisker** was sold in 1970 becoming the **Bat Snapir**. Her final name was **Hong Shen** under the Malaysian flag from 1975. As such she foundered in the Pacific Ocean on 7 November 1988. She was 900 miles off the coast of Mexico and was carrying a cargo of tyres and steel beams.

(Derek Chaplin)

The **Lady Sophia** dates from 1945 and started out as the Swedish flagged **Fernebo** for Angbats A/B Ferm, and was built to trade between the Baltic and the eastern Mediterranean. She was completed in August 1945 at Gothenburg by Lindholmens with an 8-cylinder Swedish-built Atlas diesel of 1310bhp. The **Fernebo** was 1271grt, 264 feet in length and was capable of 12 knots. In 1960 she entered the fleet of Thomas Watson (Shipping) Ltd as **Lady Sophia** under the Liberian flag, and this is how we see her at Canons Marsh, Bristol, in August 1968. In the background are two ships moored at Princes Wharf, and one appears to be a vessel of the Bristol Steam Navigation fleet. By the end of that year the **Lady Sophia** had been sold to Greek owner Keanav Shipping Co Ltd who renamed her **Chrysoula**. In 1972 she became **Olga** for George Stavrou & Nikolaos Zoulias & Co under the Greek flag and was not sold for scrap until March 1981 when she met her end at Perama in Greece.

(Derek Chaplin)

Leaving the Bristol area our next stop is at Sharpness on the Severn estuary, and also at the seaward end of the Gloucester and Sharpness Canal. The canal soon became too small to handle the increasingly larger ships, and in 1874 a large dock was constructed at Sharpness to accommodate these vessels. The import of timber products and grain became one of the main functions of Sharpness after the slump of the First World War. The elderly steam cargo ship **Lindborg** is seen at Sharpness in September 1966 with her decks packed with a cargo of timber from the Baltic. She was launched as **I.W. Winck**

on 8 November 1929 by Fredrikstad MV of Fredrikstad. As such she was 1514grt and had a triple expansion steam engine. She became **Isobel** in 1941, and then **Lotos** in 1946. She traded as **Lindborg** for D/S A/S Alf Lindo's of Haugesund and under the Norwegian flag from 1949 until January 1969, when she was sold for breaking up at Greåker, which is located inland from Fredrikstad in Norway. This elderly steamship visited Sharpness on a number of occasions towards the end of her career.

(Derek Chaplin)

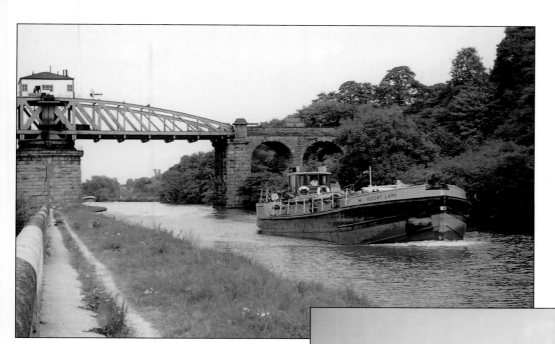

The Gloucester and Sharpness Canal starts out at the north end of Sharpness docks and proceeds towards Gloucester. Tank barges were a common sight on the canal in the 1950s and 1960s, and a fairly typical example is the **Regent Lark** seen approaching Sharpness from Gloucester, and passing the remains of the Severn railway bridge. This structure was closed to rail traffic on 25 October 1960, after being struck by the tank barges **Arkendale H.** and **Wastdale H.** which had earlier collided off Sharpness in thick fog. The canal itself was completed in 1829 and had taken nearly 33 years to construct. It was eighteen miles long and was primarily built to serve Gloucester with imports of coal and cereals such as corn and wheat, as well as timber from the Baltic. The **Regent Lark** was built in 1951 by W J Yarwood and Sons, of Northwich, for the Regent Oil Co Ltd, London. She was 104grt and measured 91 feet in length by 18 feet wide and was propelled by a 3-cylinder Ruston and Hornsby four-stroke diesel. She was sold in 1963 by which time Regent Oil had become part of the Texaco empire. She became the **Delta Lark** of N.V. Diesaf of the Netherlands, but her ultimate fate is unknown.

(John Wiltshire)

Heading inland along the canal we reach Gloucester docks. The tank barges belonging to J Harker Ltd, of Knottingley, were intended to supply refined products to inland terminals by penetrating the many inland waterways routes that existed throughout the United Kingdom. Much of their fleet was built in the 1950s in Harker's own shipyard at Knottingley, and one of the smaller examples was **Helmsdale H.** of 1955. She was built by her owner and launched on 15 September 1955. She had a gross tonnage of 105 and was powered by a 5-cylinder Gardner engine. In this view she is seen passing through the Llanthony swing bridge from the main basin at Gloucester docks and heading back into the canal on 4 June 1962. The large warehouses in the background were used for storing corn in sacks, while also visible in the left of this view are the British Waterways buildings and some interesting road vehicles. The **Helmsdale H.** will pass the old oil terminal in Monk Meadow Road and then the new terminal at Quedgeley which opened two years earlier in 1960. We now retrace our steps along the banks of the Severn to Severn Beach and await the ferry.

(John Wiltshire)

Enoch Williams was a Welshman who inaugurated a new ferry service at Old Passage between Beachley and Aust pier on 6 July 1926, and it ran until October 1928 using a 48 foot motor launch named **Silver Queen**. Not withstanding the initial failed attempt, he set up the Old Passage Severn Ferry Co Ltd a few years later and began operating on 18 May 1931 with a new wooden hulled vessel, **Princess Ida**, that was built locally. In 1934/35 expansion took place and two new steel ferries, the **Severn Queen** and **Severn King** were delivered from Beverley in Yorkshire. The vessel in this shot is the much newer **Severn Princess** built at Hull in 1959. She was twin-screw and powered by two Leyland diesels and could carry 18 cars and 94 foot passengers. Looming behind her is

the Severn road bridge still under construction in this January 1965 view taken from Aust pier near Severn Beach. This new bridge would open on 8 September 1966 and the Old Passage ferry crossing would cease. The **Severn Queen** and **Severn King** were eventually scrapped, but the **Severn Princess** was sold for further service on the west coast of Ireland. She worked out of Galway after long periods of inactivity, involved with salvage work and filming. She was re-discovered in the late 1990s in poor shape, and rescued by a charity formed by the people of Chepstow. She was returned to the Chepstow area and an attempt was made by volunteers to restore her. In 2009 she lay in a very sorry state having been taken ashore in Chepstow.

(Derek Chaplin)

Having crossed the Severn estuary the first port we encounter as we enter South Wales is Newport. Clan Line's **Clan Maclaren** is captured on film approaching Newport on 20 April 1976 where she is arriving with general cargo. She was the second vessel in the fleet to have carried this name, and sadly despite being in good condition, her days were numbered. When launched in September 1946 she was the first of a new class of six ships for her owners following the end of the Second World War. Four would be completed as motor ships and two with steam turbine propulsion. Her builders, Greenock Dockyard Company, of Greenock, delivered her as a 6021grt single screw motor ship which featured for the first time, goalpost masts between No.2 and No.3 holds. She would be followed into service the following year by the steam powered **Clan Maclachlan** from the same yard. The third member of the Clan Maclaren class was the motor ship **Clan Maclean** also delivered in 1947. The **Clan Maclaren** was powered by a 6-cylinder Doxford oil engine built by Barclay, Curle & Co which gave her a maximum speed of 15 knots. In 1976 she passed to Seymour Shipping Ltd, of London, for one final voyage to Asia for which she was renamed **Seemoor**. In May 1977 she arrived at Gadani Beach for dismantling.

(Nigel Jones)

The *Mahout* was one of a pair of motor ships delivered to T & J Brocklebank Ltd in 1963 from Alexander Stephen and Sons Ltd, of Glasgow. The *Mahout* and sister *Markhor* were the first diesel-powered ships for Brocklebank since the early 1920s and also introduced a new style of ship to the fleet. Both were 6867grt and were 480 feet in length overall. The *Mahout* had a 7-cylinder Sulzer main engine of 10000bhp assembled by her builder, and introduced bridge-control of the engine to the fleet for the first time. Entering service with a traditional black hull, she later went on to receive a white hull as seen here at Newport in December 1976, and she was in port to load packaged tin plate for the Asian continent. Incidentally *Mahout* is a Hindi name for a person who drives an elephant. After just fifteen years service the *Mahout* was sold in 1978 to Premier Maritime Inc and registered in Piraeus with the new name *Aglaos*. In 1980 and still under the Greek flag she became *Evagelia S.* for Myrica Shipping Corp. Unfortunately she was badly damaged on 11 September 1982, 25 nautical miles from Bandar Khomeini, Iran, after either being hit by Iraqi aircraft or striking a mine. She was later refloated and confiscated by Iranian authorities.

(Nigel Jones)

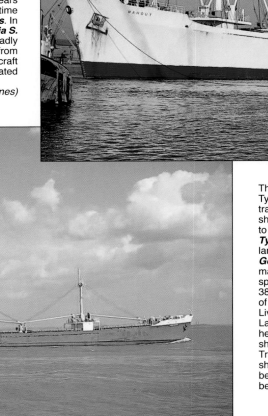

The Burnett Steamship Company was founded in 1889 in Tynemouth with the newly-built vessel *Angelus*, and initially, trading was to London and northern Europe. In excess of forty ships were to be operated over the years until the fleet was sold to Canadian owners in 1962. Post-war ships included the *Tynemouth* of 1955, the tramp ship *Holmside* of 1959, and the larger single-deck bulk carrier *Gosforth* of 1962. The 5836grt *Gosforth* was built by Hall Russell, of Aberdeen, and had her machinery positioned aft. She was 410 feet long and had a speed of 14 knots; her main engine was a 6-cylinder Sulzer 3840bhp diesel. She was a four-hold ship with a grain capacity of 365,100 cubic feet and was employed on trading from Liverpool and Glasgow to Canada which would include the St Lawrence Seaway and the Great Lakes. The *Gosforth* is seen here sailing from Newport in September 1969. Four years later she was sold and became the *Thorold* for Quebec and Ontario Transportation Co Ltd sailing under the Canadian flag. In 1985 she changed her name to *Catherine Desgagnes*, and was believed to be still in existence in 2010, but her future was becoming uncertain with the arrival of newer tonnage.

(Danny Lynch)

The Swedish built **Vinni** was typical of many bulk carriers that were to visit Newport in the late 1960s and throughout the 1970s. We see her making her way into the lock on the afternoon tide of 25 May 1968, with the Newport Screw Towing tug **Dunosprey** working at her aft quarter. The tug had not long entered service at this time. The **Vinni** was a large vessel of 22124grt and 38130dwt and was launched in September 1966 by Gotaverken at Gothenburg for Norwegian owners S/A Eidsiva Smatank of Oslo. Her dimensions were 657 feet in length by 89 feet breadth and she had seven holds that had been strengthened to cope with heavy cargoes such as iron ore. Cargo handling gear consisted of five modern electrically powered cranes and a substantial enclosed crows nest can be seen on her foc'sle. She was powered by a 7-cylinder A/B Gotaverken diesel of 12050bhp and was capable of 16 knots. Earlier in 1968 while underway from Rotterdam to Hampton Roads the **Vinni** was involved in the rescue of 24 people from the distressed Canadian vessel **Charny**, which later sank. She became the **Aegis Storm** in 1974 and the Panamanian **Chi Star** for Chi Star Navigation S.A. in 1979. As such she was finally to meet her end at Kaohsiung in October 1984.

(John Wiltshire)

The **Navelinacore** was one of a class of sixteen refrigerated cargo ships built between 1964 and 1971 in three different Norwegian yards for Maritime Fruit Carriers of Haifa, Israel. The first four vessels were built with Israeli Government subsidy and as such had a limited military capacity. Many of these reefers sailed under the Israeli flag while a number were managed by Maritime Fruit Carriers but flew the West German flag. The **Navelinacore** delivered in 1970 was one such example, that sailed for F.M. Atlantic Frigomaris Kuhlschiffreederei GmbH & Co Ltd. She was one of nine built by Bergens M/V in Oslo and had a grt of 8190, being identical to the **Sultanacore**, **Clementinacore** and **Pecancore**. These were fast ships at 19 knots, powered by a 7-cylinder Akers / Nylands Verksted B&W engine of 11500bhp. In 1975 the **Navelinacore** briefly became the **Navelina**, and in 1976 the **Pasadena**. Her final guise was as the **Citrus do Brasil** for Brazilian owners and sailing under the Liberian flag from 1992 until 2003. In May 2003 she arrived at Alang in India to be scrapped after an impressive thirty-two years service. She is seen at Newport on 28 October 1972 when just over a year old, and wearing the funnel colours of Swedish company Salen Shipping.

(John Wiltshire)

Prior to the opening of the new tidal harbour at Port Talbot in 1970, the supply of iron ore to Llanwern steel works arrived at Newport in what seemed like a continuous procession of ore carriers. Amongst these ships were a number operated by Scandinavian fleets including the 18735grt **Livanita**, which we see at Newport on the lay-by berth on 5 July 1972. She was the first of two similar ships built in the UK by Smiths Dock Co Ltd of South Bank, Middlesbrough, for A/S Ugland Rederi, of Grimstad in Norway. When delivered in March 1962 the **Livanita** was placed on a fifteen-year charter to the British Iron and Steel Corporation (BISCO). She was powered by a 4-cylinder Doxford P type oil engine and was capable of 13 knots. She had three main cargo holds (two at 162 feet and one at 81 feet in length), with five Velle-type hatches. The **Livanita** was sold in 1978 shortly after her BISCO charter expired, and became **Vida**, sailing under the Liberian flag for Cement Carriers Corp, of Monrovia. At this stage we must assume that she became a cement carrier, but after only six years she was renamed **Hoppet** in April 1984 for Delrin Shipping Co, of Gibraltar. On 24 August 1984 she was delivered to Chinese ship breakers at Ningbo.

(John Wiltshire)

Built at Dundee by the Caledon Shipbuilding and Engineering Co, the 10203grt motor ship **Stentor** was delivered in 1946 to the Ocean Steamship Company. She had, however, been ordered along with her sistership **Rhexenor** for the Ministry of War Transport and the **Stentor** was completed at a cost of £673,000. She had a 6800bhp 8-cylinder Burmeister and Wain diesel built in Scotland by John G Kincaid which gave her a service speed of 15 knots. In 1958 she was transferred to Glen Line as the **Glenshiel** and five years later reverted to the name **Stentor** sailing for another associated company China Mutual Steam Navigation. At 28 years of age the **Stentor** was still going strong and in 1974 took up work on Elder Dempster routes for Ocean Steamship. She finally left the Ocean Group in 1975 when her name was modified to **Tento** for a six-day delivery trip from Singapore to Taiwanese breakers. She is seen waiting for a berth at Newport on 13 July 1968.

(John Wiltshire)

The unusual looking **Kingsnorth Fisher** was the second of two specialist extra heavy-lift carriers, the first such vessels in the world. They were diesel-electric, twin-screw ships constructed in 1966 for charter to the Central Electricity Generating Board by owners James Fisher & Sons Ltd. The **Kingsnorth Fisher**, built by Hall Russell at Aberdeen, was named after the power station on the River Medway, and she was followed into service by the **Aberthaw Fisher** (built by Ailsa at Troon). Both vessels were designed with the intention of carrying large items of electrical generation plant such as transformers which would remain on the road transport whilst on board. Three such items weighing up to 300 tons each could be transported by these ships, which had shallow draughts so they could reach remote berths possibly close to power stations. They featured a hydraulically operated lift-platform aft for use at quaysides, a bow-thruster unit and full bridge control of engines, ballast pumps and all major deck machinery. The **Kingsnorth Fisher** is seen underway in Newport docks in November 1968. She became the **New Generation** in 1990 whilst her sister **Aberthaw Fisher** became the **National Generation**. The latter was sold in 1996 to be converted into a dredger. The **New Generation** was retained by James Fisher and Sons PLC, and finally sailed to Indian breakers in late 2001 as the **New Gen**.

(Danny Lynch)

The 7463grt cargo ship **Herefordshire** was launched at Sunderland on 16 February 1972 for Bibby Line being delivered to them in June 1972. She was followed into service four months later by the identical **Lancashire**. Her builders were Doxford & Sunderland Shipbuilding & Engineering Co who installed one of their 67J6 opposed piston slow-speed oil engines giving her a speed of 16 knots. The two sisterships were used to trade worldwide in a tramping capacity and could be seen virtually anywhere from Japan to Mexico as well as occasional visits to UK waters. The **Herefordshire** had an overall length of 529 feet and her cargo handling facilities included a Stülcken derrick. After only ten years service with Bibby Line, she became **Texas** in 1982 for Brittany Shipping Corporation, of Monrovia, and three years later became **Brooklyn** for Panamanian owners. She later suffered an engine room fire in a position 19.36N/62.31E on 13 March 1986 while on a voyage from India to Romania. She was subsequently towed to Pakistan, and after being declared a total loss arrived at Gadani Beach for scrapping that October. Her sistership **Lancashire** survived her by only two years. This view of the **Herefordshire** was taken on 7 November 1976 when she was on the timber berth in the South Dock. She had arrived with a part-cargo of hardwood from the Far East.

(John Wiltshire)

The Norwegian bulk carrier **Holthorn** is discharging on the East Quay iron ore berth on 12 July 1969. She was built in West Germany in 1964 and was a large vessel for Newport docks with a deadweight tonnage of 29690 and length of 631 feet. Passing in the foreground and returning to the tug berth is Newport Screw Towing's **Dunheron** of 1955. She had been purchased the previous year from Tees Towing and was previously named **Golden Cross**. She was built by Scott & Sons of Bowling and had a 750bhp Crossley two-stroke diesel engine. The **Dunheron** was bought to replace a steam tug and was normally kept as the spare tug at Newport. She passed to Cory Ship Towage in 1971 when Newport Screw Towing sold out, and was transferred to Belfast shortly after this. After several further owners, in 2010 she still survived in a semi-preserved role, and having reverted to her original name **Golden Cross**. The bulk carrier **Holthorn** was sold by her owners SAMEIET Holthorn in 1977 to Cebaco Compania Naviera S.A. of Greece and became the **P.S. Palios**. She was broken up in Taiwan in early 1987.

(John Wiltshire)

The **Newport** was the first motor tug to appear at the South Wales ports when she was delivered to the British Transport Commission in 1956 from W J Yarwood's yard at Northwich. Until then the BTC had operated a fleet of steam tugs at Cardiff, Barry and Newport including well-known vessels like **The Earl** and **Gwent**. By 1963 BTC tug operations at Barry and Cardiff ceased leaving a fleet of three tugs to serve internal dock movements in Newport. The **Newport**'s owners became restyled as the British Transport Docks Board in 1963 and she lost her black hull by 1968 in favour of the livery she carries here. By the 1970s she was generally regarded as the spare dock tug at Newport, her 700bhp output and single-screw propulsion being a handicap. On 3 April 1972, however, the **Newport** is seen hard at work as the bow tug on the bulk carrier **Polinnia**. After several failed attempts, the BTDB eventually surrendered their towing operations at Newport in 1977. Included in the deal were the two 1960-built twin-screw motor tugs **Llanwern** and **St. Woolas**, but not the **Newport**. She was put up for sale and in 1978 sailed for new owners in Egypt and has not been traced.

(John Wiltshire)

The **Waveney** was a Dutch-built coaster, one of a pair of similar ships owned by Blue Star Line Ltd in the 1960s, and both managed by Gillie and Blair Ltd, of Newcastle. The **Waveney** together with her sister **Orwell** had previously been named **Waveney Star** and **Orwell Star** respectively, after being purchased in 1964. In addition two new larger coastal vessels, the **Deben** and the **Crouch** were purchased in 1966, and all were used as feeder ships for the Line's main services, and operated out of London to the continent and to the Tyne, Tees and Humber ports. The **Waveney** had been launched on 25 June 1956 by Gebr. Bodewes Scheepswerven "Gruno" at Foxhol as the 487grt **Orient** for Rederij Vebo of Groningen. She had a 6-cylinder M.W.M. diesel of German manufacture and was 169 feet in length with a draught of just over 11 feet. This view of her was taken at Newport on 26 October 1969 and she is believed to be laid up at the time, with her sister **Orwell** lying close by but out of view. She was sold in 1969 to Greek owners D.P. Kalkassinas and became the **Meropi** in 1970. In 1971 she was sold on to further Greek owners, and by 1985 was sailing as **Stelios A.** for Stelios Amorgianos. Further name changes were to follow, and as late as 2006, she was still believed to exist under the Bolivian flag as the **Geneos** for Wave Shipping.

(John Wiltshire)

Things could often get very busy at times in Newport docks in the 1960s and it was not unusual to find several vessels moored at the buoys in the South Dock awaiting a berth. These would usually be ore carriers, but on 18 August 1968 we see the fine looking Scandinavian cargo ship **Augvald** unladen and waiting for an opportunity to load steel products from an adjacent quay. The **Augvald** was completed in 1958 by Uddevallavarvet of Uddevalla in Sweden for Ships A/S Corona, H.M. Wrangell and Co A/S of Haugesund and was 8609grt. She was a conventional shelter deck motor ship, with five cargo holds and accommodation for eight passengers. She was 467 feet in length and was powered by a Gotaverken diesel of 6550bhp giving her a speed of 15 knots. In 1969 she became the **Hoegh Augvald** for S/A Corona and in 1978 the **Tania** under the Singapore flag sailing for Gemini International S.A. Her final days were as the **Tania Tres** for the same owner from 1981 until scrapping at Kaohsiung in April 1984.

(John Wiltshire)

Ship towage to and from the seaward side of the lock at Newport was undertaken by Newport Screw Towing until 1971. The tugs available were reduced from five to four in 1965 with the sale of the **Duneagle**. The fleet then consisted of two Empire type steam tugs and a pair of motor tugs bought new in 1962. They would all berth at the south end of the North dock opposite the dry docks. When visiting the docks on a weekend, the first sign of any shipping movements would be if tugs were missing from their berths. On a warm summer afternoon on 9 July 1967 we see the **Dunfalcon** of 1941 and the second of the two motor tugs **Dunsnipe**. The **Dunfalcon** was built as the **Empire Pine** by Scotts

of Bowling and worked on the Clyde for 15 years as **Vanguard** and **Battleaxe**, before coming to Newport in 1961. The **Dunfalcon** was 252grt and had a triple expansion engine of 1000ihp. She was sold for scrap locally in December 1968 and broken up by John Cashmore shortly afterwards. The **Dunsnipe** was built at Hessle by Richard Dunston, and passed with the business to Cory Ship Towage in 1971 becoming **Gwentgarth**. She had a 6-cylinder two-stroke British Polar engine of 1300bhp, and was sold to Greek owners in 1980 as **Adamastos**. As such she was eventually broken up in the Piraeus area during 1987.

(John Wiltshire)

Twelve miles further down channel is the port of Cardiff. The **Tenadores** of 1960 was one of six attractive refrigerated cargo ships built by Bremer Vulkan Schiffbau of Vegesack for deployment within the Fyffes Group. The **Tenadores** was built for Surrey S.S. Co Ltd of Bermuda and was 6716grt. In her early years she was a familiar sight at ports such as Avonmouth and Southampton, but she did trade worldwide. She was built principally for the banana trade, and was transferred to Empresa Hondurena de Vapores S.A. in 1965, and placed under the Honduras flag along with three of her sisterships. This view of her dates from 26 August 1975, and she is seen making the final approach to the Channel dry-dock at Cardiff for an annual survey. A number of vessels of this class visited South Wales for dry-docking in the 1970s. The **Tenadores** had two De Laval geared steam turbines which gave her a speed of 17 knots. The year 1980 was to be her last, as she arrived at Kaohsiung for scrap on 27 January.

(John Wiltshire)

The *Swat* was quite a revolutionary ship when she was delivered new as *Wimbledon* in April 1958 to Watts, Watts and Co Ltd, of London. She was followed into service by her sistership *Weybridge*, both from the shipyard of Barclay Curle and Co Ltd, Glasgow. The design of her hull is interesting and incorporates fins just forward of the propeller and very pronounced hull knuckles both forward and aft to damp out pitching movement at sea. Crew accommodation was of a very high standard, and single cabins were arranged along galleries the full length of the midship superstructure, whilst officers were located in the bridge house. In 1960 the *Wimbledon* was chartered to Port Line amd was renamed *Port Wimbledon*, a role which she performed until 1965 when she reverted to her original name. We can see in this view taken at Cardiff on 10 April 1973, that the *Swat* has four goalpost masts which serve her seven cargo holds, one of which is aft of her machinery space. Her gross tonnage was 9223 and her engine was a 6-cylinder Doxford diesel of 6700bhp giving her a speed of 17 knots. Together with her sistership *Weybridge* she was sold in 1967 to the Pakistan National Shipping Corporation and renamed *Swat*. As such she visited South Wales, Cardiff in particular, on a number of occasions, and was eventually broken up at Karachi in 1982.

(John Wiltshire)

Ellerman Lines has its roots in 1892 when it was formed to take over a Liverpool based shipping company with twenty-two vessels. The business expanded such that by 1914 the Ellerman Group controlled four subsidiary companies and by 1939, they had 105 ships. The fine looking *City of Chester* was a wartime new-build for Ellerman Lines Ltd of Liverpool. She was launched on 30 December 1943 by Barclay, Curle and Co of Glasgow as their yard number 694. She was completed as a 8030grt twin-screw motor ship and was registered in Glasgow. Her two 4-cylinder main diesel engines were built by Barclay Curle & Co, and had a combined output of 9000bhp giving her a speed of 16 knots. By 1953 she was employed on the UK to South Africa service and would call in the Canary Islands on her outward and return trips. She is seen at Cardiff on 10 August 1969, her trading days then coming to an end. She was sold for scrap in 1971 and renamed *Chester* under the Panamanian flag for her delivery voyage to Whampoa near Hong Kong for breaking up.

(Bob Allen)

The *Petros* was a British-built cargo ship of 2046grt sailing under the Cypriot flag and was registered in Famagusta. When she was photographed sailing from Cardiff on 25 August 1969, she appeared to be a well-kept ship. She had previously arrived at Cardiff with a cargo of pit props from Archangel and was now heading for that Arctic port once again. The *Petros* was launched by Smith's Dock, of South Bank, Middlesbrough, on 20 August 1948 as the *Mabella* for Norwegian owner A/S Mabella (Karl Bruusgaard), of Drammen. She was powered by a 4-cylinder compound steam engine of 2000ihp which gave her a speed of 11 knots. In 1959 on completion of a new ship she was sold to Teesdale S.S. Co Ltd of Middlesbrough and became the *Highliner*, and in 1964 transferred to Tynedale Shipping Co with Clarke S.S. Co Ltd, of Montreal, as managers. They sold her in 1966 for around £75,000 to Cypriot owners by whom she was given the name *Virgin Mary*. She eventually became *Petros* the following year when Cypriot shipowner Pasparo Shipping took her over after paying just £40,000 for her. The *Petros* was to return to Cardiff on 20 January 1971 but in a very sorry state. She had caught fire whilst moored on the Tyne and received considerable damage amidships. Fully laden, she was later towed to Cardiff with a heavy list to starboard, and here she was discharged and then laid up in the Queen Alexandra dock. On 12 June 1972, the *Petros* made the short trip under tow to Cashmore's yard at Newport for scrapping.

(John Wiltshire)

The Yugoslavian flag **Bitola** has the very elegant lines of an Italian-built vessel and is quite modern looking for her year. She was built by Riuniti Adriatico at Monfalcone being launched on 7 May 1947 as **Adria** for Swedish owners. At 1684grt, her owners Rederi A/B Svenska Lloyd, of Gothenburg, had specified a four-hold cargo ship of 284 feet overall length, and she was powered by an 8-cylinder Fiat diesel of 1800bhp. In 1963 she passed to Atlantska Plovidba as the **Bitola** and was registered in Dubrovnik, which is how we see her at Cardiff in about 1966, making her way towards the Queen Alexandra lock without the aid of tugs. She will sail from Cardiff and head up channel to Bristol to complete the discharge of her cargo. In 1968 she became **Taras** for Cia. de Navegacion Portland and sailed as such under the Panamanian flag. In 1971 she was trading as **Indian Ocean** before making her final name change to **Dimitris K** in 1973. Six years later, and at 32 years of age, she was to meet an unfortunate end. She foundered in a position 36.24N/24.34E in the Aegean Sea on 20 December 1979 and was lost.

(Bob Allen)

The **Regent Royal** was a regular visitor to Cardiff in the 1960s with refined products. In this view she is moored at the Regent wharf on 9 May 1967. A fairly traditional looking motor tanker, she was launched at Blythswood's Scotstoun yard on 18 January 1954 and delivered to Trinidad Leaseholds Ltd, of London. The **Regent Royal** was built to carry petroleum products from that company's Pointe-a-Pierre refinery in Trinidad to the United Kingdom. The Regent brand was used to market their products in the UK and eventually both Trinidad and Regent passed to Texaco. The **Regent Royal** was 10024grt and 14405dwt with an overall length of 516 feet. Main propulsion was from a 4-cylinder opposed-piston Doxford oil engine of 4500bhp built by D Rowan and Co. Her accommodation included facilities for twelve passengers and featured a nursery. Visits to Cardiff were to end in 1968 with her sale to Greek owners A Halcoussis with whom she gained the name **Lorenzo**. In 1971 she became the **LSCO Trident** and was broken up in the Philippines in 1979. The newer Regent tankers **Regent Falcon** and **Regent Eagle** continued to visit Cardiff for a number of years, and eventually gained Texaco identities.

(John Wiltshire)

At thirty-three years of age the Greek flag **Adamastos** was surely nearing the end of her useful life - but not quite. Completed in 1935 as **Baron Renfrew** for the Kelvin Shipping Co Ltd, of Ardrossan, (associated with H Hogarth & Sons Ltd), she was a steamship of 3724grt with a triple expansion engine of 1900ihp. Built by D & W Henderson at Meadowside on the Clyde, she was 401 feet long by 53 feet in the beam. She became **Adamastos** in 1961 in the ownership of Avlis Shipping Co S.A. under the Greek flag. She is seen here on 25 April 1968, passing through the passage that links the Queen Alexandra Dock to the Roath Dock, and heading for the Spillers berth to load grain. In 1970 she became **Despina A** for other Greek owners, and lingered on for a further three years until May 1973. She was then sold to Tuber Celik Sanayii A.S., of Istanbul, and broken up at the Golden Horn later in 1973.

(John Wiltshire)

The tanker **Agios Vlasios V** is seen at Cardiff in November 1969 in rather dramatic lighting conditions. She was a steam turbine tanker built in 1956 by the Mitsubishi Zosen K.K. yard at Nagasaki in Japan. She was powered by a pair of Mitsubishi turbines of 15000shp and was capable of an impressive 17 knots. The **Agios Vlasios V** is believed to be the widest vessel ever to enter Cardiff docks. With a gross tonnage of 20140 and an overall length of 659 feet, it was her beam of 88 feet and 3 inches that was cause for concern. The lock at Cardiff is just 90 feet wide. Her stay was prolonged due to damaged machinery, and she was waiting for some new bearings to arrive from Japan. Ownership of this vessel is a little less clear. It would appear that the **Agios Vlasios V** always flew the Liberian flag, and from 1956 until about 1981 she was always managed by Chandris (England) Ltd, but had at least three owners during this time starting with Mariblanca Navegacion S.A. when delivered. By 1982 she was sailing for Eighth Kambos Shipping Corp, of Monrovia, and was sold for breaking up at Kaohsiung in August 1982.

(the late T W Wiltshire)

The Rea tugs **Butegarth** and **Tregarth** share this scene with the **Cardiff Queen** and in the background Port Line's **Port Sydney** on 28 April 1967. The location is at the west end of the Queen Alexandra dock and at this time this was the regular berth for the tugs. The P & A Campbell paddle steamer was actually laid up and moored at right angles to the quay. She had been taken out of service on 21 September 1966 and would never sail again. The **Port Sydney** was a twin-screw refrigerated cargo ship dating from 1955 and with a gross tonnage of 9189. She featured a 70 ton heavy lift derrick and was sold in 1972 for conversion into a passenger ship and eventually renamed **Daphne** in 1975. Under this name she sailed for a number of different owners and flew the Panamanian and later Liberian flag until 1996, when she was sold to a Swiss company and became **Switzerland**. By 2002 she continued in use as a cruise ship and had become the **Ocean Monarch** for Ocean Cruise Corp of Panama. She was later laid up for sale, and became the **Princess Daphne** in 2008. Rea's tugs passed to Cory Ship Towage in 1970, not long after the **Tregarth** had departed for a new life in the Caribbean. The **Butegarth** served in the Bristol Channel until 1989.

(John Wiltshire)

Lyle Shipping Co Ltd, of Glasgow, had three ore carriers built for them between 1959 and 1962 for charter to the British Iron and Steel Corporation (BISCO). The third and largest example was the **Cape Howe** which was launched on 31 May 1962 by Lithgows, of Port Glasgow, and completed in November of that year. She was time chartered to BISCO for fifteen years and would be employed bringing iron ore to the UK from locations such as Seven Isles, Monrovia, Narvik and Vitoria. The **Cape Howe** was a motor vessel powered by a 6-cylinder Burmeister & Wain diesel of 6410bhp built locally in Greenock by John G Kincaid. She had a deadweight tonnage of 27941 and was 608 feet in length with a laden draught of 32 feet 5 inches. In 1968 management of the Lyle ships passed to the Scottish Ship Management Ltd, of Glasgow, and vessels eventually gained new funnel colours that incorporated a blue lion. In January 1971 the **Cape Howe** was badly damaged in heavy seas, being hit by an abnormal wave whilst on a voyage from Port Cartier, Canada, to Immingham. Repaired, she continued to serve her owners until 1978 when she was sold to Albion Maritime Inc, of Monrovia, and placed under the Singapore flag as **Al Tawwab**. Her final voyage was from Osaka to Zhejiang in China where she arrived for breaking up on 5 February 1984. She is seen being turned in the Queen Alexandra Dock on 11 July 1969, and was a regular visitor to both Cardiff and Newport.

(John Wiltshire)

Bank Line's **Forresbank** was one of around eleven general cargo ships built for them by Wm Doxford at Sunderland between 1960 and 1963, and followed on from eight similar ships delivered between 1957 and 1959. However, Bank Line dual sourced their new-builds, and went to Harland and Wolff at Belfast for a further sixteen general cargo ships in the 1957 to 1963 period. The **Forresbank** was launched at Doxford's Pallion yard on 6 February 1962 and was completed the following May. She had an overall length of 487 feet and was 6201grt. Power was understandably a Doxford oil engine, a 4-cylinder opposed piston type of 6640bhp. Most Bank Line vessels were registered in London but the **Forresbank** was one of a small number to use Glasgow as port of registry. Built

purely for tramping worldwide, she would serve her owners until 1978 when she passed to Cypriot owners who named her **Veesky**. Three years later she was renamed **Admiral** still under the Cypriot flag and in 1983 Indian breakers purchased her for demolition at Alang. This view of her taken on 24 May 1978 shows her underway at Cardiff during her last few months with Bank Line, having paid a visit to discharge some general cargo. Of note is the lack of tug support in the dock system, due to a local strike by tugmen. This was indeed a bold move by the pilot to sail a vessel of this size from Cardiff without tug assistance.

(Nigel Jones)

The dry dock facilities at Cardiff attracted some very interesting ships over the years, and Bailey's Bristol Channel Ship Repairers were obviously very competitive when it came to attracting new business. In 1977 at least two cross channel ferries belonging to Townsend Thoresen visited Cardiff for attention. They certainly stood out in port being brightly painted passenger vessels in a more usual run of tankers and reefers using the dry dock facilities. The **Viking Venturer** was one of a class of four similar ships delivered to Townsend Thoresen between 1975 and 1976. She was built by Aalborgs Vaerft A/S in Denmark in 1975 for service between Southampton and Le Havre. In 1985 she was rebuilt at Bremen, and gained an extra car deck which resulted in a rather top-heavy and not particularly attractive profile. In 1987 ownership passed to P&O European Ferries and two years later she was renamed **Pride of Hampshire**. After serving on the Portsmouth to Le Havre service for many years in 1994 her route was altered to Portsmouth to Cherbourg, after P&O chartered the two former Olau Line ferries for the Le Havre services. After sale in 2002, she was managed by El Salam Maritime Transport of Egypt and was sailing under the Panamanian flag as the **Pride of Al Salam 2**. She was still trading in 2009 as the **Oujda** and remained under the Panamanian flag.

(John Wiltshire)

This passenger excursion vessel started life as the **St. Silio** for the Liverpool and North Wales Steamship Co. Ltd, registered in Liverpool, she was to be their only motor vessel. Completed by Fairfield at Govan on the Clyde the **St. Silio** was delivered to her owners in May 1936 and put to work in North Wales running from Llandudno, Menai Bridge and Amlwch. She spent her war years based on the Mersey and in 1945 re-entered civilian use as the **St. Trillo**. She had a gross tonnage of 314, was 149 feet in length and was a twin-screw vessel powered by a pair of 6-cylinder Crossley two-stroke diesels which gave her a service speed of 13 knots. Her two funnels gave her an elegant profile, but the forward stack was a dummy and served no purpose. The Liverpool and North Wales Steamship Co Ltd ceased to trade in 1963 and the **St. Trillo** passed to Townsend Bros Ferries Ltd to be operated by P&A Campbell, and would continue to sail from North Wales with the occasional appearance in the Bristol Channel. She is seen on her last sailing from Cardiff on 27 September 1969. Her engines were by now giving cause for concern, and the **St. Trillo** was later laid up at Barry in one of the old graving docks. In 1972 ownership passed to Nigel Wait of Surrey and in 1975 she was renamed **Thrillo**, passing to breakers in Ireland in the spring of that year. She left Barry under tow for Dublin on 21 April 1975.

(John Wiltshire)

In the 1960s Russian ships began to appear in the Bristol Channel with increasing frequency, and many of them arrived with timber from the Baltic ports. One such vessel was the **Salekhard** which was one of a class of 85 similar vessels with four cargo holds. She was built for the U.S.S.R. Northern Europe Shipping Company in 1965 and was 4846grt. There was always plenty to observe on an average visit to Cardiff docks and this shot taken on 5 October 1969 shows two crew members of the **Salekhard** at work painting the hull of their ship. Of particular note is the green boot-topping on the hull and the ice-breaker bow. The craft they are using seems to be ideal for the job, but probably not that seaworthy. It is difficult to imagine just what Health and Safety would make of this practice in 2010. The **Salekhard** was built at Gdansk in Poland and was eventually sold in 1989 to Uniforce Shipping S.A. as the **Uniforce** and flying the flag of St Vincent and the Grenadines. She caught fire in March 1993 and was subsequently scrapped at Gadani Beach later that year.

(John Wiltshire)

Dredging methods were to change quite dramatically at the South Wales ports in the 1960s. By tradition, steam-powered bucket dredgers were popular for use at ports such as Swansea, Cardiff and Newport. The **Taff** of 1946 was built for the Great Western Railway Company and named after the main river in Cardiff. She passed to the British Transport Commission in 1948 when it assumed control of the South Wales ports and was owned by the British Transport Docks Board from 1963. The **Taff** was built by Fleming and Ferguson, of Paisley, and was not self-propelled, her boiler only supplying steam to drive her bucket chain and auxiliaries. She was 607grt and 192 feet in length, and usually worked with the steam hopper barges **Ebbw** and **Usk**, both of which dated from 1948. By the time this view was taken of her, berthed in the Bute East Dock on 28 September 1969, her working days in South Wales were over. The **Taff** would be sold in 1969 together with the **Ebbw** and **Usk** to a contractor on the Thames for a few years use before being scrapped. The last bucket dredger to operate in South Wales was the self-propelled **Abertawe** of 1947 which after a period of inactivity was sold to Italian owners in 1972.

(John Wiltshire)

The **Nicolas Bowater** made just two visits to Cardiff, once in 1969 and then again in 1970, on both occasions for attention in the Bute dry dock. She is seen in the Queen Alexandra Dock on 5 June 1970, her Brunswick green hull colour and deep cream upper-works, making her a very distinctive sight. Bowater Steamship Company commenced trading in 1955 and ordered two new steam turbine cargo ships, the **Margaret Bowater** and **Sarah Bowater** from the Denny shipyard at Dumbarton. These would be for the service from Corner Brook Mill in Newfoundland to the UK and were ice-strengthened. They were specially designed as newsprint carriers, and their officer and crew accommodation was of a very high standard. They were joined in 1958 by the similar

Nicolas Bowater which would become the flagship of the fleet. Six smaller motor ships also joined the fleet between 1958 and 1961. Initially the vessels were managed by Furness Withy, but this role later passed to Cayzer Irvine from 1962. The **Nicolas Bowater** was 6875grt and 419 feet overall length. She had steam turbines assembled by her builder which gave her a speed of 14 knots. She was sold in 1973 becoming the **Vall Comet** of Vall Cargoships Ltd and sailed under the Liberian flag. Five years later on 2 June 1978 she arrived at Gadani Beach for breaking up, after two decades on the high seas. Bowaters ceased to trade as ship owners in 1977 with the sale of the 3866grt **Nina Bowater** of 1961, the last new ship purchased by the company.

(John Wiltshire)

The Union Castle Mail Steamship Co had taken delivery of a pair of refrigerated cargo ships, the **Roslin Castle** and **Rochester Castle** in 1935 and 1937, and they were followed during the latter part of the Second World War by a further three similar size ships, all five being motor vessels. A sixth vessel was the **Riebeeck Castle** which appeared in 1946 followed the same year by the final vessel in the series, the **Rustenburg Castle**. All seven ships were to be found employed on the mail service to South Africa, and would carry fruit on the northbound voyage to Europe and general cargo on the outward run to South Africa. These ships were regular visitors to Cardiff, and the **Riebeeck Castle** is seen here on 26 June 1971 underway in the Queen Alexandra Dock. Her gross tonnage was 8342 while her service speed was about 16 knots and she was completed by Harland and Wolff at Belfast. Not long after this photograph was taken she left European waters for the last time bound for Taiwan, arriving at Kaohsiung on 2 September 1971 for breaking up.

(John Wiltshire)

The Panamanian flag cargo ship **Locarno** is seen as she is about to take up a berth in the Queen Alexandra Dock in Cardiff on 14 April 1971. It is only a temporary move as she will eventually move to the Roath Dock to load grain at the Spillers wharf. This fine looking vessel has a triple expansion steam reciprocating engine which was supplied by G. Clarke & N.E. Marine Ltd and had an output of 1275ihp. She was built in 1956 by Austin and Pickersgill at Sunderland as the **Helmwood** for Wm. France Fenwick and Co Ltd of London, and is still in more or less original condition. She had a gross tonnage of 3403 and an overall length of 344 feet. In 1968 she became **Locarno** for Cia. De Nav. Ponto Ronco S.A., who then renamed her **Paula II** in 1975. She passed to Criterion Maritime Corp S.A, Panama in 1977 as **Smile** and was eventually broken up at Vado Ligure in early 1979. In this photograph the **Locarno** is carrying the funnel colours of Tsavliris Shipping, of Piraeus. Of note on the quayside is the photographer's Lambretta scooter, which played an important role in many random visits to Cardiff docks, often in lunch hours or on the way home from work.

(John Wiltshire)

The **Suevic** was a fine looking passenger cargo liner of 13587grt, operated by Shaw Savill and Albion Line and built by Harland and Wolff at Belfast in 1950. She was a twin-screw vessel, 561 feet in overall length, powered by steam turbines and capable of 17 knots. Together with her sistership **Runic** also of 1950, she was employed on the service between the UK and Australia and New Zealand carrying refrigerated meat and dairy produce as well as general cargo. The **Runic** had a short life as she was wrecked on 19 February 1961 on a reef 120 nautical miles from the Lord Howe Islands, during a hurricane. The **Suevic** continued in service until 1969 when she spent a short period in lay-up. Back in service, she continued to trade until 1974 when, after major engine damage, she was sold to Taiwanese breakers at Kaohsiung. This shot of her was taken at Cardiff on 10 May 1972 as she makes her way up the Queen Alexandra Dock, to take up her berth on the Empire Wharf adjacent to the cold store warehouse.

(John Wiltshire)

49

HMS Flying Fox is seen lying on the foreshore at Cardiff in April 1973 having arrived for breaking up by Birds of Cardiff, whose scrapyard was just a few hundred yards away inland. The end of this ship would commence when she was deliberately set on fire, having a large content of wood in her construction; this was intended to simplify her demolition. The *Flying Fox* had been built in 1918 for the Royal Navy by Swan Hunter on Tyneside. She was a Class 24 single-screw, 17 knot minesweeping sloop, all of which were named after racehorses. In 1920 she passed to the Royal Naval Volunteer Reserve and was decommissioned. She was then rebuilt in 1923 as a training ship and the floating headquarters for the Bristol Division of the RNVR. She took up her new role in 1924 based at Hotwells in Bristol, and after the Second World War the volunteer unit became known as the Severn Division. In 1972 the RNVR moved into new shore-based premises given the name **HMS Flying Fox** and the hulk *Flying Fox* was declared surplus to requirements. In March 1973 she was sold for scrap, and prepared for her short voyage across to Cardiff, her first in 49 years. She was towed away from Bristol on Sunday 18 March.

(Bob Allen)

The **King George V** was to become a resident at Cardiff for nearly seven years, a story though with an unfortunate ending. She was built in 1926 by Wm. Denny, of Dumbarton, as a passenger steamer for Turbine Steamers Ltd and William Buchanan, of Glasgow. She received new boilers in 1935 and later that year ownership passed to the London Midland and Scottish Railway, in association with David MacBrayne Ltd, and was put to use working out of Oban. The **King George V** took part in "Operation Dynamo", the evacuation of Dunkirk in the Second World War, and after refurbishment was back in service from Oban in 1947. By 1973 she was working for the newly-formed Caledonian MacBrayne and was withdrawn in September 1974. She passed to C H Bailey of Cardiff in April 1975 and was laid up in one of the Mountstuart dry docks at the Pier Head. She is seen here approaching the dry dock on 22 April 1975, which would be her resting place until June 1981 when she was sold to the Bass Charrington group. The plan was to renovate her for use as a static pub/restaurant on the River Thames. While being refurbished she caught fire on 25 August 1981 in the Bute dry dock, and was badly damaged. The **King George V** was quietly towed around to the foreshore of Tiger Bay in 1984, and broken up by Birds of Cardiff.

(John Wiltshire)

The Strick business can be traced back to 1885 when Frank C Strick set up as a shipbroker and coal exporter based in London. From the early days the company traded to the Persian Gulf and by the turn of the century had three offices in South Wales at Newport, Cardiff and Swansea. Strick Line was sold in 1919 to Gray Daws and Co who in turn sold it on to P&O subsidiary The Hain Steamship Co Ltd in 1923. It continued to be operated as a separate entity, and the *Tangistan* was one of the new builds to enter the fleet in the early post-war years. She was completed in June 1950 by John Readhead & Sons Ltd, South Shields, and was one of the last steam ships completed for Strick. Readhead was Strick's preferred builder and in 1953 completed their first motor ship for

the company, the *Balistan*. Powered by a triple expansion engine incorporating a low pressure turbine, the *Tangistan* was a single screw ship of 7383grt and 458 feet in length. She ran builder's trials on 23 June 1950 before being handed over to her owners, and went on to serve Strick Line for nearly twenty-two years before being sold to Taiwanese breakers in 1972. She arrived at Kaohsiung for beaching and demolition by Tung Seng Steel Co on 13 March that year. In happier times the *Tangistan* is photographed passing Penarth Head outbound from Cardiff in May 1969. The beach below the headland offered a good vantage point for photography, especially of vessels departing as they had usually "let go" of the tugs by this stage.

(Bob Allen)

Moving along the foreshore at Penarth we come to the esplanade and the pier. The photographer has been lucky enough to capture the Cardiff-based tug *Butegarth* as she is about to pass close to the end of Penarth Pier, outbound from Cardiff in December 1967. In the background can be seen the *Lowgarth* of 1965 and following behind, the smaller Dutch-built *Tregarth* of 1958. The *Butegarth* was the first of four similar tugs delivered in 1966 to R & J H Rea Ltd for use at Cardiff and Barry, and they would see the demise of the last of the steam tugs at these ports. Based loosely on the design of the *Lowgarth*, the *Butegarth* was delivered from her builder Richards at Lowestoft in January 1966. She had a bollard pull of 14 tonnes provided by an 8-cylinder Blackstone engine of 850bhp driving a fixed pitch propeller in a steerable Kort nozzle. In 1970 she gained the colours of Cory Ship Towage and by 1979 had become a Newport-based tug. Ten years later the *Butegarth* was the first of the quartet to be sold, passing to Arklow Shipping Ltd in Ireland as *Avoca*. A year later she has passed to Portuguese owners as *Lutamar* and was still at work in Portugal in 2009.

(John Woodward)

Passing around Lavernock Point and heading further down channel past Sully we come to Barry. Between 1963 and 1965 W Bruns & Co, of Hamburg, took delivery of nine fast refrigerated ships that were all constructed in German yards. They had 280,000 cubic feet of cargo space available for bananas plus additional space for eight other different kinds of refrigerated cargo. The lead ship was the **Brunshausen** delivered in 1963 and sold three years later. Other names included the **Brunsbüttel** and the **Brunskoog** both of 1964. In 1966 a further similar pair arrived, the **Brunshoeft** followed by the **Brunstor**. Both were built at Emden by Rheinstahl Nordseewerke and were 4639grt. They could provide a speed of 21 knots made possible by a M.A.N. diesel of 9600bhp. In 1970 the

Brunstor went on time charter to Geest Industries and is seen here sailing from Barry in Geest colours on 1 August 1970. It should be noted that W Bruns had chartered several vessels to Geest on a number of earlier occasions. In 1975 W Bruns & Co sold these two sisterships to the Russian fleet U.S.S.R. Zapryba and both received very similar new names. The **Brunstor** became the **Dneprovskiy Liman** while the **Brunshoeft** became the **Dnestrovskiy Liman**. At this time they were apparently re-classified from reefers to general cargo ships. Both were eventually scrapped in the 1990s, the former **Brunstor** meeting her end at Alang in 1996.

(John Wiltshire)

The **City of Adelaide** was an elegant looking refrigerated cargo vessel delivered to Ellerman Lines in January 1964 for their Australian service. She followed on from earlier slightly smaller ships such as the **City of Glasgow** and **City of Eastbourne** adopting the three-quarters aft layout for her machinery space. The **City of Adelaide** had five cargo holds plus a number of deep tanks for the carriage of special oils and liquids. At 10511grt she was constructed by Barclay, Curle and Co, of Glasgow, with a 9-cylinder 2-stroke Sulzer main engine of 14200bhp. This was assembled by her builder who also installed four diesel generators for supplying auxiliary electrical power. With a main engine of this size, a service speed of 18 knots was available. The **City of Adelaide** is seen laid up in the No. 2 Dock at Barry in November 1971 and not long before she went on charter to the Hamburg South America Line as the **Cap Cleveland**. By 1973 she was back in service with Ellerman Lines as the **City of Canterbury** and continued as such until sold in 1976 to Cie. Maritime Belge of Antwerp. Under the new name **Rubens** she remained a familiar sight in northern Europe for a further seven years. In 1983 she passed to Crisela Ltd as the **A.L. Pioneer** and was delivered to Bangladesh breakers in August of that year.

(the late T W Wiltshire)

One of the many sand and aggregates dredgers operating in the Bristol Channel in the 1980s was the **Peterston** of 1961. She was originally operated by the Bristol Sand and Gravel Co Ltd, of Bristol, until that fleet became part of British Dredging Aggregates by 1978. The **Peterston** was built by Ailsa Shipbuilding Company, of Troon, (yard no.511) and was powered by a 5-cylinder British Polar diesel of 810bhp. She was a suction dredger with a gross tonnage of 748 and an overall length of 175 feet, and was built with a single cargo hold. She is seen wearing the colours of British Dredging Aggregates Ltd who operated a number of other dredgers in South Wales at this time including the **Bowqueen** and **Bowcross**. The **Peterston** is photographed slowly making her way into Barry on 25 April 1986, laden with sand and with plenty of new paintwork. Visible in the distance is the village of Sully and Sully Island just offshore. In September 1987 British Dredging took delivery of the brand new, modern and much larger sand dredger, the **Welsh Piper**, which soon led to the redundancy of the **Peterston**. She was eventually laid up and scrapped at Newport docks in the early 1990s.

(Bob Allen)

Seen arriving at Barry to load coal on 29 April 1973, and without the aid of tugs, is the elderly cargo ship **Eleftherios** which dates from 1929. Her hull appears to be in very poor condition, but she is still an attractive vessel with a particularly interesting and distinctive looking wheelhouse. She is owned by Elias E Tomboulis of Greece and has a gross tonnage of 2546. She was completed in December 1929 as the **Barmbek** for Knohr and Burchard Nfl, of Hamburg. Her builder was Flensburg Schiffsb. Ges, of Flensburg, who completed her as a 2446grt vessel with a compound steam engine. In 1949 she became the **Kate Grammerstorf** and in 1950 she returned to her builder to receive a new forward section, which is when her gross tonnage rose to 2546. Her overall length for the remainder of her days would be 332 feet while her beam remained at 45 feet. She retained her steam engine until 1957 when she was fitted with a 2000bhp diesel of Deutz manufacture, and in 1965 she became the **Eleftherios** under the Greek flag. As the **Eleftherios** she passed from Tomboulis to a Mr Stavrou in 1976, who removed her engine for use in another vessel. The hulk was then sold to M Spiliopoulos and was eventually broken up at Perama in late 1977.

(John Wiltshire)

The Liberty ship **Rodos** makes a lasting impression as she sails from Barry in 1967 on her final voyage. She had loaded a consignment of scrap metal at the port and would depart for China where she too would be reduced to scrap. Liberty ships were built in the United States during the Second World War. They were based on a British design and were cheap and quick to build. In all no fewer than 2710 were built between 1941 and 1945 at eighteen different ship yards. The **Rodos** was launched on 6 September 1943 by Todd-Houston, of Houston, Texas, and completed as **Erastus Smith**. She was a standard Liberty ship with a gross tonnage of 7244, and had a General Machinery Corp. triple expansion steam engine which gave her a speed of 11 knots. In 1947 she became **Kyma** for Livanos Bros sailing under the Greek flag. She gained the name **Rodos** in 1960 when she passed to Orient Shipping Corp who placed her under the Lebanese flag. Upon arrival in China she would be discharged and subsequently delivered to ship breakers at Shanghai who would scrap her by September 1967. In 2010 it would appear that two Liberty type ships still survive in preservation.

(Bob Allen)

The cable laying ship **John W. Mackay** was truly a survivor when seen here in the No.1 Dock at Barry in January 1972. She was in port for repairs which included fitting a new boiler. The **John W. Mackay** was built in 1922 by Swan Hunter and Wigham Richardson on the Tyne for the Commercial Cable Company of London. She was 4080grt, 360 feet in length and had a pair of triple expansion steam engines of 3300ihp. Her twin screws gave her a service speed of 14 knots and her hull was strengthened for operation in ice. Having replaced an older vessel she was put to work maintaining cables across the North Atlantic until the onset of the Second World War. After a spell based in Nova Scotia, she was taken over by the Admiralty and put to work laying cables in the Pacific, eastern Mediterranean and Persian Gulf. She resumed her duties in the North Atlantic after the war and following the refit in 1971 mentioned above, she ventured to new areas such as Australasia. In 1977 she was finally retired and laid up on the Thames at Greenwich. Despite much interest in her, including proposals to include her in a new Museum of the Docklands, the elegant looking **John W. Mackay** would not work again. She remained at her moorings and in 1990 was moved to the River Tyne at Hebburn for possible preservation. Sadly the end came in 1994 when she was towed away to Aliaga in Turkey for breaking up.

(Bob Allen)

The two steam tugs **Caroline Davies** and **Emphatic** make a fine sight moored up near the main lock at Barry, and awaiting their next turn of duty. The date is unknown but must be no later than 1962. The **Caroline Davies** is indeed an elderly tug, built way back in 1909 as the **J. O. Gravel** by A McMillan and Son, of Dumbarton, for The Sincennes-McNaughton Line Ltd, of Montreal, Canada. She returned to the United Kingdom in 1916 as the **H.S.45** for service with the War Office. After a period on the Manchester Ship Canal as **Clarendon** she came to the Bristol Channel in 1952 and entered service at Cardiff with J Davies Towage as **Caroline Davies**, being sold for scrap in 1962. Alongside is the 1943-built **Emphatic** built as the **Empire Joan** by Cochranes at Selby for the Ministry of War Transport. She became **Emphatic** in 1947 with the Admiralty and based at Chatham. As **Emphatic** she came to the Bristol Channel in 1958 when purchased by Edmund Handcock, of Cardiff, passing to the Bristol Channel Towage Co in 1960. In 1963 R & J H Rea Ltd took over all towage operations at Cardiff and Barry and included in the deal was the **Emphatic** which went on to become the **Hallgarth**. She was scrapped in 1966 at Newport, her role taken over by a more efficient motor tug.

(Derek Chaplin)

Gibbs and Co was a small South Wales shipping company with an office in Newport. The size of its fleet varied but was never more than about three ships. The **Welsh Troubadour** was delivered in April 1974, the last in a series of three Sunderland-built SD14s delivered to subsidiary company Welsh Ore Carriers Ltd between 1973 and 1974. The two earlier ships were the **Welsh Endeavour** and **Welsh Trident** and were all completed by Austin and Pickersgill. The **Welsh Troubadour** was 9201grt and had a 5-cylinder Clark-NEM Sulzer main engine giving her a speed of 15 knots. She is seen in the dry dock at Barry receiving her annual survey on 16 September 1978. She became **Welsh Jay** two years later and **Silago Express** in 1986. Remarkably in March 1997 she returned to Newport, her original home port, as **Navira Express**, with a cargo of animal feed. After twenty-three years service, and bearing the name **Rena One**, a Calcutta breaker's yard was to be her final resting place in September 1997. Her demolition was swift, being completed by 9 November.

(John Wiltshire)

Crusader Shipping Co Ltd traded between New Zealand, the Far East and the Pacific coast of North America, and was owned equally by four well-known shipping companies; these being Shaw Savill & Albion Line, Port Line, Blue Star Line and the New Zealand Shipping Co. They began trading in 1958 with three new ships, the *Crusader*, the *Saracen* and the *Knight Templar* which were all managed by Shaw Savill and Albion, and were later joined by one ship from each of the other three partners in the Crusader venture. The ship seen in the above photograph, the *Langstone*, was built in 1958 by Valmet of Helsinki as *Saracen* and was 3441grt. She was a refrigerated cargo ship with four holds served by 8 derricks. She was powered by a 10-cylinder Gotaverken diesel of 6250bhp and could achieve 17 knots. Leaving Crusader Shipping she passed to Shaw Savill in 1970 and in 1971 gained the name *Langstone* as seen here. She later became the *Dimitrios K* in 1974 for Greek owners, Triakapa Shipping S.A. and was broken up at Bombay in 1981. Standing out from other shipping by virtue of her light green hull, she is seen at Barry on 3 September 1972 on charter to Geest Industries.

(John Wiltshire)

In 1955 the Falkland Islands Dependencies Survey (later to become the British Antarctic Survey) sought a replacement for the vessel **RRS John Biscoe** (of 1944) and found a suitable ship in Norway. She was the small passenger/cargo vessel **Arendal** that had been launched in 1954 for Norwegian owner Arendals Dampskibsselskab and completed in February 1955. She was built by Solvesborgs Varv of Solvesborg, Sweden, and had a gross tonnage of 994 and a single cargo hold. The **Arendal** was purchased and converted into a research vessel and renamed **Shackleton**. She was built to operate in ice and had a 6-cylinder M.A.N. engine and a controllable-pitch propeller. In 1957 she struck an iceberg off the South Orkney Islands and was slightly damaged. She became **RRS Shackleton** in 1968, and was then allowed to fly the blue ensign, frequently undertaking scientific cruises to the Antarctic. She continued her role as a survey ship and oceanographic scientific laboratory latterly with the Natural Environment Research Council, until 1983. The **RRS Shackleton** was then sold to Hydrosphere becoming **Geotek Beta** and later **Profiler** in 1984. She is currently sailing as **Sea Profiler** for Gardline Marine Services and flying the Panamanian flag. On 11 July 1976 we see her arriving at Barry as the **RRS Shackleton** (the RRS is not shown on her bows though).

(John Wiltshire)

Naval vessels would occasionally visit the South Wales ports on courtesy calls and more often than not would stay in port for a number of days during which they would be open to the public. The frigate **HMS Zulu** (F124) was one of the Royal Navy's seven strong Tribal class. She was launched in July 1962 from the Govan yard of Alexander Stephen and Sons and was commissioned on 17 April 1964. She was the third Royal Navy vessel to carry the name **Zulu**, which is that of a South African tribe. **HMS Zulu** was the only Tribal class frigate to be built with Seacat missiles, her class sisters being fitted with these at a later date. After fifteen years active service she was put into reserve in 1979, and despite being placed on the disposal list in 1981, the Falklands War in 1982 saw her re-commissioned and put to service in the Home Waters fleet. The following year she became the Gibraltar Guardship, an ancient role in which a warship is acting in a defensive role, against a Spanish invasion of the Rock. In June 1983 she is seen here making for the lock at Barry after a brief visit. 1984 was her last year under the White Ensign as she was sold to the Indonesian Navy with two other members of her class **HMS Gurkha** and **HMS Tartar**. **HMS Zulu** was to become the **Martha Kristina Tiyahahu**.

(Bob Allen)

Port Talbot lies at the mouth of the River Afan in Swansea Bay. The British Iron and Steel Corporation (BISCO) specified a total of 73 ore carriers that would be taken on either ten or fifteen year charter, the first ship being completed in 1953. They would be built to three different sizes and would be owned by several shipping companies and consortia. The smallest size ore carrier was the "Port Talbot" type of which there were twenty-four vessels. The hull dimensions of 427 feet length and 57 feet beam were restricted by the size of the lock at Port Talbot. Vessels of this size, however, were also ideal for taking cargoes to Irlam Steelworks on the Manchester Ship Canal as well as serving the Cumbrian port of Workington and General Terminus quay in Glasgow. The *Clarkeden* and her sister *Clarkavon* were a pair completed by Short Bros, of Sunderland, for H Clarkson & Co Ltd, of London, and managed by the Denholm group. The *Clarkeden* was completed in 1958 and had a gross tonnage of 6861 and she is seen arriving at Port Talbot on 16 January 1970. Within the Denholm group a number of similar looking vessels could be found sailing with subsidiary Scottish Ore Carriers. At the end of her fifteen year charter in 1973 the *Clarkeden* was sold to Phaedon Shipping Co. S.A. of Panama as *Phaedon* and flew the Greek flag. In her final guise as *Berane* she was sold to Yugoslav breakers at Split in April 1982.

(John Wiltshire)

Sailing from Port Talbot on 22 September 1969 is the traditional motor coaster *Olivine* belonging to William Robertson Shipowners Ltd, of Glasgow. She was launched in December 1951 by Ailsa Shipbuilding Co Ltd, of Troon, and delivered in February 1952, She was intended for United Kingdom coasting and trade to the near continent. The *Olivine* featured a raised quarter deck and had three hatches. She was 244 feet overall length and 38 feet in the beam and had a gross tonnage of 1353. Her main engine was a 2-stroke British Polar diesel of 1310bhp. The *Olivine* became *Lisa* in 1976 which was under the Greek flag and operating for G Stavrou, E Malkogiorgis and Co. Having foundered in a position 36.55N/11.44E near Pantelleria, an island close to Sicily, on 28 October 1976, her seagoing days came to a rapid close. Behind the ship is the once very popular beach and seaside resort at Aberavon. The classic funfair, amusement parks and weekend crowds have long gone.

(John Wiltshire)

The German flag freighter **Arnis** was an ore carrier built in 1959 by Lithgows of Port Glasgow as **Morar**. She was owned jointly by her builders and Scottish Ore Carriers. Morar is the name of a village in the West Highlands. She had a gross tonnage of 6990 and was the first British vessel to be propelled by a "free-piston" gas turbine, and also the first cargo ship in the world to be built as such. This space saving arrangement incorporated a Pescara type exhaust gas turbine supplied with gas from three free-piston gasifiers supplied by the Free-Piston Engine Company. The output power was in the region of 2500 shaft horse power which gave the **Morar** a speed of 11 knots. This installation was modified in her first year with the addition of a fourth gasifier unit. Her cargo holds were fitted with Erman's patent rolling steel hatch covers, another first. The **Morar** became **Clari** in 1967 for Reederei Barthold Richters of Hamburg. At this point her unusual power installation which proved to be a disaster, was removed and replaced with a more conventional 9-cylinder diesel of 4000bhp made by Werkspoor N.V. The **Clari** became the **Arnis** in 1969 and she was fitted with a set of modern cargo derricks. After a short spell under the Cypriot flag she passed to Indonesian owners who renamed her **Mahoni** and used her for carrying a variety of cargo. As such she foundered on 26 September 1979 off the west coast of Taiwan. She was later refloated and then broken up at Kaohsiung in Taiwan by Chai Tai Steel & Enterprise during late 1980. The **Arnis** is seen at Port Talbot on 22 January 1971, and is waiting to discharge a cargo of iron ore.

(John Wiltshire)

The Alexandra Towing Co did not normally buy second-hand tonnage, but in 1966 a thirteen-year-old motor tug became available, and with a need to replace elderly steam tugs at Swansea and Port Talbot, the **Caedmon Cross** of 1953 was purchased. She was from the Wm. Crosthwaite (Tees Towing) fleet at Middlesbrough and had been built by Scott and Sons at Bowling on the Clyde. Alexandra Towing named her **Margam** and based her at Port Talbot, which is where we see her, adjacent to the dry dock entrance on 19 July 1968. She was a handy size tug for working in the restricted lock at Port Talbot, but at 750bhp, not a particularly useful tug at Swansea. The **Margam** was sold in 1970 to Willem Muller, of Terneuzen, in the Netherlands who renamed her **Rilland** and replaced her Crossley engine with an 8-cylinder Brons of 1000bhp in 1971, and fitted a smaller funnel. She sank in the Bay of Biscay approximately 150 miles west of St Nazaire on 22 November 1989; fortunately her crew of three were saved.

(John Wiltshire)

The Commissioners of Irish Lights performed a similar role in the Republic of Ireland to that of Trinity House in the United Kingdom. The operation was a lot smaller and at any one time, included a number of light vessels as well a couple of tenders. One such tender was the twin-screw steam engined **Isolda** of 1953. She was built as a buoy and lighthouse tender by Liffey Dockyard Ltd in Dublin and was 1173grt and 233 feet overall length. She had a pair of triple expansion engines of 1500ihp driving two screws and capable of 12 knots. She is seen sailing from Port Talbot on 30 January 1970 having delivered a lightship to the port for dry docking. She became **L.E. Setanta** (pennant number A15) in 1976 having been purchased by the Department of Defence in Dublin, for use by the Irish Naval Service. She was armed with two single 20mm Oerlikon guns and used as a training and supply ship for a number of years. Her end came in 1984 when she was sold to Haulbowline Industries at Passage West for breaking up.

(John Wiltshire)

Two of the Port Talbot size ore carriers were built in France and were more or less identical. They were the **La Colina** for Buries Markes Ltd, of London, and the **Philippe L.D.** for Louis Dreyfus et Compagnie, of Paris. Both were completed in 1958 by Chantiers Réunis Loire-Normandie, of Grand Quevilly, near Rouen. Both vessels had a pair of 8-cylinder Deutz diesels geared to a single propeller shaft and a speed of 12 knots. The **Philippe L.D.** was 6733grt and had a small freight hold in addition to two main cargo holds. Her initial disposal was to Salvesen Offshore Holdings Ltd in 1974 as **Soutra** and later **Gullane** in 1975. She was converted into a drill-ship at North Shields between late 1974 and June 1976. Her profile changed completely and she was fitted with new diesel-electric propulsion and given the new name of **Dalkeith**. She was renamed **Wingate** in 1976 for City Drilling Services before reverting to **Dalkeith** once more in 1978. In 1980 she was operating for the Danish company J L Offshore Drilling as **Dan Baron** and now flying the Bahamas flag. The final chapter of this second career for the old **Philippe L.D.** was with Norwegian owners as the **Viking Explorer** from 1987 until 7 September 1988. On this day she sank in the Makessar Strait seventy miles north of Balikpapan following a large natural gas explosion. The **Philippe L.D.** is seen moored on the iron ore discharge wharf at Port Talbot on 12 June 1969. This was the original berth and could handle two vessels at a time.

(John Wiltshire)

The new deep water tidal harbour at Port Talbot was officially opened by Her Majesty the Queen on 12 May 1970. The harbour was built to handle much larger bulk carriers than could previously be accommodated in the existing enclosed dock system. The main destinations for imports would be Port Talbot and Llanwern steelworks sites which would receive imported iron ore and later coal from the new facility. Ship owner C T Bowring was established in 1841 and was involved in sealing, tramping and later tankers. In 1965 they formed the Seabridge consortium along with Hunting, Houlder Bros, Silver Line and H Clarkson. The **Sydney Bridge** was a large bulk carrier completed in September 1970 by Harland and Wolff at Belfast and followed on from the Dutch built **Forth Bridge** and **London Bridge** of 1967, being somewhat larger, at 31093grt. The **Sydney Bridge** had

an overall length of 735 feet and was 106 feet in the beam which meant that Port Talbot would be the only port in the Bristol Channel she could visit at that time. She had seven cargo holds and would be used principally for the carriage of iron ore. She is seen arriving at the new Port Talbot harbour on 18 May 1971. The new harbour was a major construction project and upon completion would require a considerable amount of dredging to keep it open to large bulk carriers. Meanwhile Bowring pulled out of the Seabridge consortium in 1978 and the **Sydney Bridge** was sold, becoming **Amorgos** under the Greek flag. In 1981 she became **Bontrader** for Hemisphere Shipping Co Ltd and was eventually broken up at Alang, arriving there in February 1997.

(John Wiltshire)

Another river to flow into Swansea Bay is the Neath, which does so just below Briton Ferry. The **Monica D.** had arrived at Briton Ferry on 31 July 1972 having previously visited Avonmouth to discharge her final cargo. She was a Swedish-built general cargo vessel completed at the end of the Second World War by Oresundsvarvet at Landskrona. She was actually launched in 1942 as **Hermund**, but was laid up incomplete, being finished off for her Norwegian owners Hermund, Skibs-A/S Oilexpress (Sigurd Herlofsen & Co), of Moss, in August 1945. She was a motor ship with a speed of 14 knots and gross tonnage of 4936. In 1950 she changed her name to **Black Condor** when she began to sail for Black Diamond Line, and from 1957 was managed by Herlofsen and Hvattum of Oslo. She became **Hermund** again in 1962 and was sold in 1965 to Egil Naesheims Rederi-A/S, of Haugesund, and renamed **Vardal**. She was finally sold to Italian interests in December 1968 and became **Monica D.** sailing under the Panamanian flag for Black Diamond Navigation Co S.A. By the time this view was taken on 24 August 1972, she had lost most of her masts and derricks and it would only be a matter of time before demolition began.

(John Wiltshire)

The refrigerated cargo ship **Marrakech** flew the Moroccan flag and was one of the last ships to arrive at Briton Ferry for breaking up. The **Marrakech** was a relatively small ship with an overall length of 340 feet and a gross tonnage of 3214. She was built as a fruit carrier in 1949 by Kalnes MV, of Tonsberg, as the **Ringdrude** for Skibs A/S Ringwood, Skibs A/S Ringulv and Ringdals R (Olav Ringdal), of Oslo. She had a 10-cylinder Burmeister and Wain main engine of 3400bhp and was capable of 14 knots. She became **Marrakech** in 1963 when she was purchased by Soc. Marocaine de Nav. Fruitières, of Casablanca, who were to operate her for the final fifteen years of her career. After an impressive twenty-nine years seagoing career, she arrived on the River Neath for scrapping by Thos W Ward Ltd on 20 June 1978. Nearly six months later on 9 December, she still awaited her call to the breaking berth.

(Danny Lynch)

Our final port of call is Swansea. Another type of cargo vessel built in large numbers during the Second World War was the Victory ship, which was in effect a development of the Liberty ship (see page 57). Around 530 Victory ships were built in various yards across the United States for the U.S. Maritime Commission, the first appearing in February 1944. Designed as a 15-knot ship, the Victory was in many ways superior to the earlier Liberty type. Officially designated type VC2, at 455 feet in length and 62 feet in the beam, they were powered by a double-reduction cross-compound steam turbine of 6000shp. At the end of the war many were sold and the 1945-built *Gustavus Victory* passed in 1947 to Empresa Lineas Maritimas Argentinas as *Santa Fe*. This fine looking ship was constructed by the Bethlehem-Fairfield shipyard at Baltimore, one of 94 Victory ships built at this yard, and had a gross tonnage of 7672. Twenty-four years after taking up flying the Argentine flag, the *Santa Fe* is seen arriving at Swansea on the evening tide of 3 September 1971, to load a part-cargo of locally produced steel and tin plate for South America. As could be expected her days would be numbered, but the *Santa Fe* did manage to sail for a further thirty-five months before arriving home at Buenos Aires to be withdrawn for breaking up locally.

(John Wiltshire)

69

The British-owned **Silksworth** is seen being towed out of the lock at Swansea on 1 October 1971 fully laden with a cargo of coal. She was built for R S Dalgleish Ltd, of Newcastle-upon-Tyne, and was 16553grt with an overall length of 598 feet. She took her name from a small colliery village near Sunderland. Shipowner Dalgleish operated a small fleet of ships on a variety of dry cargo trades. For example, at one time the company had two ore carriers built for charter to the British Iron and Steel Corporation (BISCO) as well as tramp ships trading worldwide. The **Silksworth** was a modern seven hold bulk carrier and was completed by J L Thompson at the North Sands yard in Sunderland in May 1964. She had a 6-cylinder Doxford main engine and was capable of at least 15 knots. The year following this view the **Silksworth** became **China Sea** for Yick Fung Shipping & Enterprises under the Somali flag and in 1976 was sold to China Ocean Shipping Co. (COSCO) as **Hua Hai**. Her fate after 1996 is unknown, but it is likely that she was scrapped in China by this date.

(John Wiltshire)

Quite a number of interesting and mainly elderly ships called at Swansea in the late 1960s and early 1970s to load locally sourced coal for export to amongst other places, southern Europe. The Panamanian *Carmelina* was a former British cargo ship that sailed for the Hudson Steamship Company of London from 1946 until 1967. Built in Scotland at the yard of the Ailsa Shipbuilding Company at Troon, she was completed in October 1946 as the *Hudson Strait*, a steam collier of 3105grt. She was similar to the slightly smaller *Hudson Cape*, also of 1946, and had a triple-expansion engine of 1380ihp. She was 337 feet in length and had a draught of 19 feet when fully laden and was followed into the fleet in 1949 by the similar *Hudson Firth* and *Hudson River*. In 1967 she became *Carmelina* for Pargomar S.A. of Panama and wore the funnel marking of Greek ship owner Tsavliris Shipping. She is seen here loading coal at Swansea on 6 January 1970 and is believed to have made several visits to the port for this purpose. At some stage in her career she has lost her two traditional masts and gained her own cargo handling gear which included a rather solid looking goalpost mast. The *Carmelina* was eventually scrapped at Vado Ligure in Italy in the summer of 1975. The Hudson Steamship Company had traditionally been involved with the coal trade between the ports in north-east England and the Thames area, but later moved into deep-sea tramping with larger ships.

(John Wiltshire)

The family business of John Kelly Ltd, of Belfast, operated a fleet of sixteen colliers in 1963, all having names beginning with "Bally". The *Ballylumford* was one of two steam colliers delivered in 1954, the other ship being the slightly larger *Ballymena*, the first motor ship did not arrive until 1958. The *Ballylumford* was completed in May 1954 by A & J Inglis of Pointhouse near Glasgow and had a gross tonnage of 1147. She was originally ordered in 1951 and it was intended to name her *Bryansford*. The *Ballylumford* was propelled by a 950ihp triple expansion engine built by Aitchison, Blair Ltd and had oil-fired boilers. In 1957 she was lengthened from 237 feet to 255 feet which increased her gross tonnage to 1242. She was sold for scrap in July 1971 along with the *Ballymena* and both were delivered to Faslane on the Clyde for breaking up, arriving on 8 July 1971. She is seen here sailing from Swansea on a fine 28 May 1971. John Kelly's vessels were a regular sight at Swansea working in the coal trade.

(John Wiltshire)

The motor tug **Cambrian** was a "one-off" and was launched on 9 February 1960 for the account of her builders Charles Hill and Sons Ltd, of Bristol, and construction work continued slowly whilst a buyer was sought. She was 163 tons gross, 94 feet in length and her engine was a reliable 8-cylinder Ruston & Hornsby of 960bhp. Upon completion and still un-named, she was eventually delivered as **Cambrian** in August 1960 to the Alexandra Towing Co Ltd, and was based from new at Swansea and Port Talbot. Here she is seen making her way into the Queens Dock, Swansea, when photographed on 20 August 1969. After only twelve years service in South Wales she was rather surprisingly sold in 1972 to Malta Ship Towage, of Valletta. She kept the name **Cambrian** until 1981, when MST was reformed into Tug Malta Ltd, and she was renamed **Mari**. Her days in Malta were over when after a period in lay-up, she was renamed **Mar** in 1996, and then sold to Turkish breakers in 1997. She was beached at Aliaga and quickly demolished.

(John Wiltshire collection)

In the 1950s and 1960s a number of conventional cargo ships were built at shipyards in the north-east of England for either Greek or Liberian owners. The **Tarpon Sea** was launched from William Gray's Hartlepool shipyard in December 1956 as the **Pearl Sea**. William Gray was the largest shipbuilder in the Hartlepool area and brought prosperity to the Hartlepools for around one hundred years. The **Pearl Sea** was completed in April 1957 for Monrovia Shipping Co. Ltd and had a gross tonnage of 8119. She was powered by a 4-cylinder Doxford engine and had a service speed of 13 knots. She is seen here as **Tarpon Sea** in unladen condition at Swansea on 15 December 1972. Of particular interest are the two crew members suspended on rope benches (called "stages") over the bow, and hard at work painting the ship's hull. Given the time of year, one would hope they did not end their working day in the dock. Having become **Tarpon Sea** in 1969 for Tarswift Shipping Co of Piraeus, she was sold again in 1975 gaining the name **Dapo Sea** for Compania Filothei S.A. of Piraeus. The end came in June 1977 for this five-hold cargo ship. While anchored at Sitra, Bahrain, she caught fire, and finished her days at Gadani Beach shipbreakers the following October.

(John Wiltshire)

The Priam Class was the ultimate development of fast cargo liner built for service under the British flag. It comprised eight ships, four of which went initially to Glen Line, the other four to Blue Funnel, and all were intended for Far Eastern service. Two of the Glen Line ships were built in Japan, while the remaining six were built on the Tyne, and were the subject of considerable delays at the shipyard. The Blue Funnel quartet were named **Priam**, **Peisander**, **Prometheus** and **Protesilaus** and they were quite simply too late in the day to demonstrate their full potential because containerisation had already arrived. Features worthy of mention are the highly automated machinery space and control room and the Burmeister and Wain diesel down rated to 18900bhp, but still capable of providing 21 knots. Cargo space was divided into 6 holds with No. 2 and No. 6 incorporating deep tanks. A 60 ton Stülcken derrick served No. 3 and No. 4 holds complemented by 5 ton derricks and electric cranes. These vessels were rarely seen in the Bristol Channel, and the **Protesilaus** makes a fine sight discharging at Swansea on 31 May 1978. The four Glen Line ships passed to Blue Funnel in 1972. The **Protesilaus** of 1967 was 12094grt and built by Vickers Armstrong Shipbuilders, of Newcastle. She was sold to CY Tung, of Hong Kong, later in 1978 and renamed **Oriental Importer**. While on a voyage from Dammam to Kuwait in June 1985 she was caught up in the Iran-Iraq War and struck by two airborne rockets and badly damaged.

(John Wiltshire)

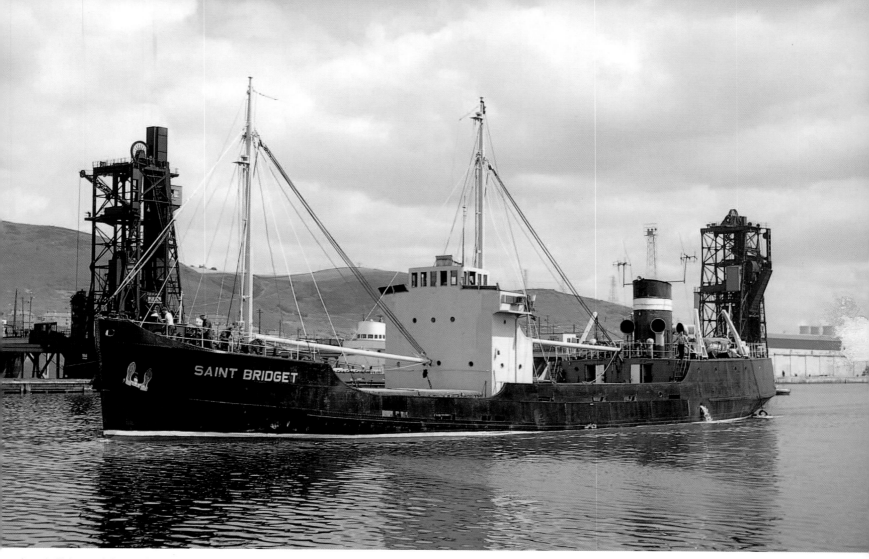

Joseph Fisher and Sons, of Newry, Northern Ireland, managed the 1953-built motor coaster **Oak** which, along with the older steamship **Palm**, was actually owned by the Newry and Kilkeel Steamship Co Ltd, also of Newry. The **Oak** was 709grt and 190 feet in length with a draught of 12 feet 6 inches and power was from a 5-cylinder British Polar oil engine. She was launched on 2 December 1952 on the Clyde and completed by Scott and Sons, Bowling, in 1953. In 1964 the **Oak** passed to J & A Gardner Ltd, of Glasgow, and was renamed **Saint Bridget**. She is in fine shape on 28 June 1969 when we see her making her way down the Kings Dock at Swansea towards the main lock. On 8 February 1972 the **Saint Bridget** was in Carrick Roads, transhipping a cargo of nitro-glycerine to the Blue Funnel cargo vessel **Autolycus** when it was found to be leaking. Being of a highly explosive nature, the cargo was considered to be very unstable and so the **Saint Bridget** was towed away and deliberately destroyed in an explosion forty nautical miles south of the Lizard peninsula.

(John Wiltshire)

Lykes Brothers Steamship Company was founded in 1898 in New Orleans, later moving to Tampa, Florida. The **Thompson Lykes** was an early example of a large class of multi-purpose cargo ships which also included **John Lykes** and **Zoella Lykes**. Their most noticeable feature was the use of twin exhaust uptakes in place of a conventional funnel. They were designed to carry a variety of dry bulk and general cargo, as well as having provision for oils and other liquid cargoes. A small refrigerated cargo hold was to be found aft of the machinery space and accommodation for up to twelve passengers was also

provided. The **Thompson Lykes** was a steam turbine propelled ship of 10186grt. She was built by Ingalls Shipbuilding Corp of Pascagoula in 1960 and powered by GEC geared turbines developing 9900shp giving her a service speed of 17 knots. She is seen at Swansea on 1 June 1970 waiting to load. The Lykes family finally sold the company to Canadian Pacific in 1997 after reaching a state of bankruptcy. As for the **Thompson Lykes**, she was lengthened in 1971 and in 1994 was converted into a barge and renamed **Lykes Enterprise**.

(John Wiltshire)

Another former Victory ship to visit Swansea was the **Kingsport**. However, she was a vessel with a very interesting history. Completed in 1944 as the **Kingsport Victory** by California Shipbuilding Corporation for the US Maritime Commission, she was purchased by the US Navy in 1950 to carry military cargoes and she was renamed **USNS Kingsport**. Eleven years later she arrived at Portland, Oregon, to be converted into a satellite communication ship. She was fitted out at considerable expense with "state of the art" electronic communications equipment including satellite tracking, a special high frequency radio station and deployment of underwater listening devices of a "sensitive" nature. She was kept busy in this role until January 1984 when she was laid up, eventually being scrapped in 1992. This shot taken on 7 June 1973 shows her arriving at Swansea in the company of the tug **North Buoy**. The **North Buoy**, new in 1959, was one of the last steam tugs built for Alexandra Towing and moved to Swansea from Liverpool in 1969. She was sold to Italian owners in 1973 and renamed **Corragioso** and eventually broken up at Brindisi in December 1988.

(John Wiltshire)

Another classic steam cargo ship visiting Swansea to load coal was the splendid French flag **Dione** of 1948. She is seen sailing from Swansea on 24 June 1969 bound for the west coast of France with her cargo of "black diamonds" and is known to have visited Swansea several times. Ordered by the French Government, she was completed by At & Ch. De Bretagne S.A. of Prairie-au-Duc, near Nantes, as **Lens** in June 1948. At some point in the same year she acquired the name **Dione** and began trading for Soc. Navale Caennaise (S.N.C.). She had a traditional triple-expansion steam engine built by At & Ch. De Loire and a gross tonnage of 2613. Her dimensions were 322 feet overall length with a beam of just under 44 feet. She was broken up during 1970 at Tamise in Belgium.

(John Wiltshire)

Built by Richards of Lowestoft in 1956 the former trawler **Ocean Crest** was a Lowestoft drifter of 131grt and powered by a Ruston and Hornsby engine. Her original owner was Bloomfields Ltd, of Great Yarmouth, and she was registered in Great Yarmouth as YH207, but by 1963 she was working for Small and Company, of Lowestoft, as LT468 and managed by Hobson's. In 1967 the **Ocean Crest** had been acquired by the University College of Swansea for use by its Department of Geology and Oceanography. She was modified and as was officially re-registered as a research and survey vessel. She is seen sailing from Swansea on an overcast 16 June 1972, and making her way out to sea to undertake survey work, possibly along the Gower coastline. She was to remain in this role at Swansea until 1984 when she appears to have been sold to Emmaledes Ltd, of Penzance, and subsequently re-classified as a fishing vessel. She was last heard of fishing once again off the west coast of Ireland in the 1990s.

(John Wiltshire)

The **Baglan** was a "state of the art" suction hopper dredger when delivered to the British Transport Docks Board's South Wales dredging fleet in 1966. She was one of three similar trailing suction dredgers delivered by Ferguson Shipbuilders Ltd, of Port Glasgow, at around this time. She featured a pair of 600hp sand pumps, port and starboard side-arms, pipes able to dredge to a depth of nearly 56 feet and one large hopper with bottom discharge doors. The **Baglan** was 1889grt, 250 feet in length and was normally based at Swansea, whereas her near sister the **Lavernock** tended to cover the ports in south-east Wales . When delivered she had a black hull, but by the time of this view on 27 June 1972 she was wearing the later BTDB colours. Her manoeuvrability was good as she was twin-screw. She had diesel electric propulsion with two electric motors totalling 1120shp. Each motor had its power supplied by a pair of Paxman 16YLCZf diesel generators with a total output of 4540bhp. The **Baglan** was transferred to work at Garston on Merseyside in the mid-1980s, and re-engined in May 1988. She was sold in 1996 when she became **Santa Ray** under the Honduras flag. She later passed to Eldemarine Ltd, of St Kitts, in 2000, and is believed to be still in service.

(John Wiltshire)

The **Clydebank** was the final member of a class of six fast cargo ships built in 1973/74 by Swan Hunter on the Tyne for Bank Line (Andrew Weir & Co Ltd.). She was constructed at their Hebburn yard and completed in July 1974. These were special vessels intended primarily for use on the UK to South Pacific service and featured cargo tanks for vegetable oils, some refrigerated capacity and the ability to take 240 containers of the forty foot variety. The **Clydebank** was 11405grt and had a Doxford 76J6 opposed-piston engine of 15000bhp. She is seen leaving Swansea on 11 May 1996 having loaded, and embarking on a positioning trip bound for South Africa. By this time it was

indeed unusual to see a general cargo ship at Swansea, let alone a British-owned example. The **Clydebank** had now been replaced on the South Pacific round-the-world service by newer tonnage, and was about to operate a new service between south and east Africa, the Arabian Gulf, India and Pakistan. This was a monthly sailing taking 56 days, which also occupied her sistership **Forthbank**. Both vessels were sold in 2000, the **Clydebank** going direct to Indian breakers at Alang after twenty-six years service with Bank Line.

(Nigel Jones)